America,
Wake Up!

"It is customary in democratic countries to deplore expenditures on armaments as conflicting with the requirements of the social services. There is a tendency to forget that the most important social service that a government can do for its people is to keep them alive and free."

Slessor

America, Wake Up!

Bill and Nita Scoggan

Royalty Publishing Company
Manassas, Virginia

Royalty Publishing Company
P.O. Box 2016
Manassas, Virginia 22110
(703) 368-9878

FIRST EDITION
Typeset by REF Typesetting & Publishing, Inc.
    Manassas, Virginia   (703) 361-2300
Printed in the United States of America

ISBN 0-910487-08-1
Library of Congress Catalog Card Number: 86-060221

Cover design by Nita Scoggan

The Dick Hafer illustrations are selected from *Secular Humanism?* ($3.95) and *Population Primer* ($3.95), published by Anastasia Press, Box 279, Stafford, Virginia 22554. Please enclose $1.00 per copy for postage and handling.

Foreword

Americans must wake up to the dangers threatening our nation—humanism, creeping Communism, and increasing terrorist activities against American people and their property. The authors recall America's Biblical heritage, our military sacrifices to protect and defend our liberties, our past victories and recent humiliations and defeats. The key to the future lies in America's Christian people.

This could be the most vital book you've read about America's past and future.

Dedicated to our children, and grandchildren, with the prayer that we may never lose the liberties which we often take for granted. Arlington Cemetary is a grim reminder that our freedoms have been obtained by the sacrifices of brave Americans.

TABLE OF
CONTENTS

Chapter 1. Taking a Long Look 5
Chapter 2. Land Of The Free 11
Chapter 3. America's Christian Heritage 15
Chapter 4. America's Christian Textbooks 23
Chapter 5. Communist Influence In Schools 33
Chapter 6. Phonics and Communism 41
Chapter 7. Public Schools—War Is Raging 49
Chapter 8. Schools Teach A New Religion 59
Chapter 9. Communism—A Mortal Challenge 65
Chapter 10. Communist Goals 71
Chapter 11. The United Nations—Haven For Spies 77
Chapter 12. Threat To Our Hemisphere 83
Chapter 13. Communism in Romania 92
Chapter 14. Twenty Wars! 99
Chapter 15. Communism in Nicaragua 103
Chapter 16. Growing Soviet Investment 111
Chapter 17. Grenada—Communism Halted 115
Chapter 18. Mexico—Communism Closer To Home 118
Chapter 19. Aspects of Deterrance 127
Chapter 20. Why Has God Allowed It? 131
Chapter 21. In Debt, Dissatisfied & Discontent 137
Chapter 22. Understanding The Times 143
Chapter 23. A Prayer For America 147
Chapter 24. There Are Answers 151

America, Wake Up!

INTRODUCTION

Rush hour traffic on the beltway around Washington, DC seemed unusually slow on July 2nd as impatient commuters, most of them federal workers, headed home after a sweltering day in the nation's capital.

WTOP radio news reported sightings of a large number of Russian ships off the Atlantic coast. Pentagon sources said Soviet authorities had announced they were coming for summer maneuvers, but Defense officials assured reporters that the Air Force and Coast Guard would keep a watchful eye on these activities.

Weary motorists who had plans to head out early for the beach for the July 4th holiday weekend faced more delays. According to the news, traffic was increasing across the Bay Bridge, with delays already up to an hour.

Later the evening news with Dan Rather featured an interview with the Secretary of State, who labeled as "routine" maneuvers the Soviet ships coming to join the Russian submarines which normally operate in the east coast waters.

The next day, July 3rd, millions of Americans were enjoying a Saturday at the beach or mountains, and few paid much attention to the afternoon news which revealed three men and one woman had been apprehended at various NATO military airfields. The suspects were caught with arms and explosives, and were believed to be involved in a sabotage plot against the NATO facilities. The suspects were being held for questioning, but had thus far refused to talk.

The seven o'clock news reported that an unidentified man had been killed in an explosion at a Pershing II missile launch site. He drove a car carrying dynamite into the head-quarters building at the missile launch facilities. No group had claimed credit for the destruction.

Suddenly . . .

Without warning, at 5:30 a.m. on July 4th, the Soviets attack the United States early warning satellites. Some are destroyed, others are malfunctioning.

America's nuclear missile submarines have been detected by Russian space stations and destroyed.

Simultaneously, Russian ships and submarines off the Atlantic and the Pacific coasts fire their missiles at highly populated coastal cities.

At the same time, Soviet intercontinental ballistic missiles flash across the North Pole enroute to their targets—Chicago, Los Angeles, Dallas, New York City, Washington, D.C., and Orlando.

Soviet bombers and fighter planes, meanwhile, have struck key military targets in western Europe, and started a massive attack against NATO command centers.

A combination of nuclear and chemical weapons are used against European cities, inflicting limited damage to areas the Soviets intend to take over and occupy.

The timetable is well planned and executed, with all of these events occurring simultaneously.

At 5:34 a.m., Eastern Standard Time, high altitude nuclear explosions disrupt America's satellite and ground communications.

One minute later, our Minuteman missiles are rendered inoperative by nuclear explosions occurring above them.

At 5:36 a.m., nuclear explosions from the first barrage of Soviet ICBM missiles destroy or cripple the North Atlantic Air Defense (NORAD) Headquarters in Colorado and the Strategic Air Command (SAC) headquarters in Nebraska.

Further explosions, at 5:38 a.m., from the first barrage of missiles inflict massive destruction upon US cities, including: Boston, Baltimore, Seattle, San Francisco, Houston, and New Orleans.

More missiles fired from Russian submarines explode on

US military targets, keeping the Armed Forces from retaliating.

America's military airfields undergo massive damage, and our planes are inoperable, and useless.

In the first ten minutes of this surprise attack one hundred million people, or more, in the United States are killed. Scores of American cities are leveled.

Fifteen minutes later, a second barrage of intercontinental ballistic missiles is fired from the Soviet Union. They streak across Alaskan skies to destroy the pinned-down Minutemen missiles in their silos and to destroy American cities.

Soviet ground forces, which have been battle-trained in Afghanistan as preparation for this takeover, move swiftly into West Germany, Italy, and Turkey, two hours after their attack on the United States.

America's military facilities and naval ports lie useless and the US is unable to transfer any forces for the defense of Europe, as the Russian war machine erupts on land and sea in a scope never before seen.

Within 24 hours, Soviet leaders demand that the United States surrender, or face the total destruction of surviving cities and industries by further missile attacks.

Thirty-six hours after their deadly worldwide operation began, the Soviets occupy the European continent, as one nation after another surrenders to the Russian ultimatum, including England.

This hasn't happened, but it could.

The infamous Pearl Harbor sneak attack would look like a Sunday School picnic compared to a deadly Soviet surprise war. Crafty Communists have succeeded in duping the United States into abiding by treaties to disarm itself, thus weakening our ability to defend and protect our citizens and property.

Communist goals for world conquest have never been secretive, nor have they changed over the years. John Lenczowski, Director of European and Soviet Affairs, National Security Council, said: "Americans are no longer aware of the danger and threat of Communism. There were a number of books exposing Communist goals and activities, in the 1940's and 50's, but today there are practically no books to alert our citizens to their deadly aims."[1]

Is there hope for America? There is—but time is running out!

You have the answers in your hand, but you must use them.

America, Wake Up! This could be the most vital book you've read. Anyone who loves America will want to share the information contained herein with their loved ones.

Chapter 1

Taking A Long Look

This nation was originally Biblically based and oriented. British law, and America's system of laws, were taken directly from the Bible. Our leaders recognized God was the law-giver and we were to enforce and abide by His laws . . . not by the changing circumstances of time, but the unchangeable laws of God. The Puritan founders analyzed issues from their basis as students of Bible law. They were able to perceive problems and deal with them because they were always interpreting life according to their basic principles.

Daniel Webster said: "If we abide by the principles taught in the Bible, our country will go on prospering . . . but if we and our posterity neglect its instruction and authority, no man can tell how sudden a catastrophe may overwhelm us and bury our glory in profound obscurity."

But America neglected and rejected the instruction and authority of the Bible, and God brought judgment. Our nation was torn apart from within by the Civil War and President Abraham Lincoln called the nation to a day of humiliation, prayer and fasting.

In his proclamation Lincoln said: ". . . Inasmuch as we know that, by His divine law, nations, like individuals, are subjected to punishments and chastisements in this world, may we not justly fear that the awful calamity of civil war, which now desolates the land, may be but a punishment inflicted upon us for our presumptuous sins . . . ?"

The President continued, "We have been the recipients of the choicest bounties of heaven. We have been preserved these many years in peace, and prosperity. We have grown in numbers, wealth, and power as no other nation has ever grown. But, we have forgotten God . . . intoxicated with unbroken successes, we've become . . . too proud to pray to the God that made us!"

The pattern that developed was one of people not remembering the Biblical principles upon which this nation was founded, so they had no way of evaluating their conduct. Having given up the basis for telling good from evil, they could no longer discern the difference—and war was upon them.

The World War I hero, Alvin York, said in 1941: "The things people forget is that freedom is so precious we don't just fight for it once and stop." Yes, the price of freedom is eternal vigilance.

After WWI God sent a new adversary, Communism. Its goal—world conquest.

In 1924, Lenin said: "First we will take over eastern Europe, second the masses of Asia, then we will surround America. We will not have to fight. It will fall into our hands like overripe fruit."

Meanwhile, America began to lose her schoolchildren, as a result of forgetting God. Communism began to influence the most respected professors. One of them was John Dewey, who made many trips to Moscow for special study courses including Marxist philosophy. Dewey assisted in setting up summer schools, in Moscow for other American professors who were eager to accept these new ideas. Having rejected their Biblical source for evaluating things, they could no longer tell what was right and wrong in teaching their precious little ones.

John Dewey was acclaimed by America's scholars for his progressive new methods. Dewey's *See Dick, See Jane* look-say textbooks removed God from public classrooms. Soon, his textbooks replaced McGuffey's Readers. McGuffey's Readers were different—they were biblically oriented lessons to build godly character and values into the children.

Dewey's look-say method completely eliminated phonics and stressed sight reading, or sight-guessing. Within five years over 10,000 students couldn't read! America had her FIRST encounter with dyslexia—learning disabled children. Until that time, everyone who went to school could read!

American citizens should have insisted that those teachers be fired, but we left that decision to the intellectual experts. People felt they were not well educated enough to disagree, and surely these learned teachers must know what was best for the children.

What they didn't realise was that reading was no longer a top priority because, as John Dewey said, "Reading is a hindrance to Socialism!"

Russia, however, has never allowed anything but phonics to be taught in any of their schools . . . and their students are excelling, while America's students are floundering under National Education Association's insistence on more funds for special teachers for poor readers, but continuing sight reading versus phonics.

In this book we deal with the effect of Communism and Humanism on education. This is a vital issue because approximately 25% of the American population is involved in education! It's an enormous figure, all caught up under the shadow of a corrupt idea. In other books, we hope to deal with other issues affecting our nation. We have not, by any means, exhausted the network of corruption attacking America's institutions.

"He that walketh with wise men shall be wise, but a companion of fools shall be destroyed." Prov 13:20

God gave us wise counsel, but having discarded it, many Americans could no longer recognize their nation's enemies.

In 1936, for the first time a Communist candidate spoke to the National Press Club and received support from the nation's press who defended the Communist Party's RIGHT to campaign without hinderance.

Two Communist congressional candidates were elected

in New York in 1936. Audiences around the country were large and enthusiastic. The *Chicago Tribune* published a report that Moscow had ordered the American Communists to back Franklin D. Roosevelt.

Norman Thomas campaigned for President of the United States, his slogan: **Socialism versus Capitalism**. In January 1936, Al Smith spoke to a Liberty League Banquet warning "There can be only one capital, Washington or Moscow."

The aim of the Communists was to weaken America militarily. They supported *abolition* of Reserve Office Training Corps (ROTC), declaring: "We fight all moves of American Imperialism to build up its war machine."

In 1933, the Communist Party carried on a frenzied campaign against the Civilian Conservation Corps (CCC), accusing the government of creating *"forced labor camps"* to militarize American youth. The party made "Against the Roosevelt War Budget" one of its chief slogans for an anti-war demonstration in 1936. It continued to denounce all military expenditures well into 1937.

Americans became so accustomed to Communist ideas, they became comfortable with them. The Scriptures warned us about being joined with unbelieving atheists. But Communists became acceptable allies in all kinds of movements. It was wrong to treat them this way, but America could no longer discern—so we swallowed their poison.

A large portion of the *American League Against War and Fascism* was drawn from religious and pacifist circles! They were either willing to overlook the Communists' support of some wars, or did not realize that the Party opposed ONLY "imperialist" wars. Many Americans went along with Alexander Bittelman when he demanded: "NOT A CENT, NOT A MAN, FOR ARMAMENTS AND WAR!"

God continued to stir up enemies, from within our borders and without. Hitler's rise to power didn't come about suddenly or in a secret corner of the world. In *Mein Kampf*, Hitler told us his intentions, but we didn't believe him. We hadn't learned that others cannot be trusted.

People were so eager to have peace they let themselves

believe his protest—that his military buildup was not to rearm Germany, but merely to defend its borders. Next, people believed Hitler when he said the buildup was necessary only to obtain parity, following World War I. Then, at last, when it was too late people said: "THERE IS NOTHING WE CAN DO, BUT CONTRITELY SURRENDER."

We were totally unprepared for the war that ensued. World War II cost America a tremendous price in human lives. Pearl Harbor, Corrigidor, Iwo Jima, Bataan, and other tiny islands in the South Pacific became household words as American troops fought to preserve our liberty. But war rekindled our appreciation of freedoms often held lightly. Americans were willing to fight to keep America the land of the free and the home of the brave. Did they die in vain?

Because of our faithlessness—our failure to remember our Biblical roots—God continued to raise up problems for us.

To stop Communists in Viet Nam, Cambodia, and Laos, 58,000 Americans gave their lives. These were conflicts without official declaration of war. Discord, distrust, and demonstrations tore at the very fiber of our nation. Iran held our citizens hostage, and America waited helplessly for their release. God took away our strength and caused America to become weak, when once we were strong.

Today, a new war called PEACE is hotly raging. A Russian Presidium President said: "There will be electrifying, unheard of concessions, overtures of peace and the capitalists, stupid and decadent, will leap at another opportunity for peace. And when their guard is down—we will smash them with our clenched fists."[1]

Many naive Americans would do anything for the promise of peace. They declare: "We must disarm, or surely we will perish." The Communists clap their hands with glee when we *willingly* become militarily weak. There is something worse than going to war. There is a tendency to forget that the most important social service that a government can provide for its people is to keep them alive and free. Turning the other cheek is for the individual, not a nation.

God is using the Communists and the terrorists as a constant threat to our nation's peace and security. Increasing terrorist attacks, such as the bombing of the U.S. Capitol building, and the U.S. Navy Yard in Washington, DC have caused Americans to take a good look at defending our nation's leaders and our historic buildings. These attacks are the results of our refusal to go back to the Bible. Some people think that if we beat these enemies, we've got America's problems solved. But we don't.

We must, we must remember that it is God who has brought our enemies upon us. The Old Testament is full of examples of war and destruction upon the nation every time God's people turned from Him to serve idols. All this was written for our learning! The things we are facing today are just like those. If we recognize these patterns and begin to live according to God's Word, every enemy will become ineffective and melt away.

God is using humanists, globalists, and others to relentlessly attack the foundations of America's beliefs. If we defeat one of these enemies, God will raise up another—He will continue to do so until we learn—until we figure out what the problem is. Americans must face the fact that we are under judgment right now, and turn back to the Lord. We must rise up and be the people of God—or the judgment will get worse. America had better wake up!

God isn't through with America yet. The united cry of genuine repentance in this nation will be heard on high and answered with pardon of our national sins, restoration of peace, and blessings.

We must once again recognize that those nations ONLY are blessed whose God is the Lord.

The evidence of God's blessings for our faithfulness, and cursing for our idolatry follows. You owe it to yourself to examine the following chapters. Anyone who loves America shoud study this evidence for himself.

Chapter 2

Land Of The Free

"Blessed is the nation whose God is the Lord" is a phrase often quoted from Psalm 33:12.

Truly America has been a blessed nation, but most agree that we've become weak morally, financially, and militarily. Unable to stand against terrorist kidnapping of our citizens nor attacks on our embassies and property, we have suffered humiliation and defeat.

Why? America's founders knew the answer.

President Abraham Lincoln knew why. He called the nation to prayer and fasting at a time when our nation was torn apart from within by the Civil War. He said Americans had become: "heady with unbroken successes, we've become too proud to pray to the God that made us."

Daniel Webster said, "If we abide by the principles taught in the Bible, our country will go on prospering . . . but if we and our posterity neglect its instruction and authority, no man can tell how sudden a catastrophe may overwhelm us and bury our glory in profound obscurity."

A Frenchman visiting America said of our nation, "America is great because America is good. If America ceases to be good, America will cease to be great."

God's hand has been on America, since the days Columbus came to this new land. He wrote in his diary that he felt God was guiding him and he claimed it as territory to further the gospel of Jesus Christ. Freedom to worship brought the Pilgrims. Those settlers and founders of this nation fought sickness, hardships and increasing laws imposed by the ruler of the countries they had left . . . in order to obtain liberties they soon took for granted.

Every time Americans forgot God, He sent war.

After World World I God sent a new adversary, Communism. Its goal—world conquest.

In 1924, Lenin said: "First we will take over eastern Europe, second the masses of Asia, then we will surround America"—the last bastion of freedom. "We will not have to fight. It will fall into our hands like overripe fruit."

Many today are saying **Better Red Than Dead**. Are we willing to trade our liberty for a little temporary safety?

Secretary of Defense Caspar Weinberger said, "I don't subscribe to the **Better Red Than Dead** philosophy. How can people live in a slave society which monitors every word that's said and doesn't permit them freedom of expression, freedom of religion—and will consign them to a concentration camp or a slave labor camp?"

Patrick Henry put it very plainly, "Is life so sweet and peace so dear, as to be purchased for the price of chains?"

Behind the smiles and detente lie the Communist goals of world conquest. What have we learned from Romania, Korea, Viet Nam, Cambodia, Poland, and Afghanistan? **The price of liberty is the ability to defend and preserve it.**

We need to remember what the Communists have written about their aims: "Let the ruling classes tremble at a Communist revolution. The proletarians have nothing to lose but their chains. They have a world to win." (The Communist Manifesto).

They have not been secretive about their views and aims for world conquest.

Karl Marx said the Communist aims were to:
1. De-throne God.
2. Destroy capitalism.
3. Abolish private property.
4. Eliminate the family.

Communist goals haven't changed.

When Kruschev came to America in the 1950's and spoke to the United Nations, he took off his shoe and pounded it on the lectern to emphasize his point when he said of the United States: "We'll bury you!" He said that on American television. Millions heard it, but didn't believe it.

Millions of Americans today have had a lapse in memory, and have forgotten the Communist goals for world control.

Communists are always working toward their goals of world conquest. They are very patient. They are not concerned if it doesn't happen this year, or next year. They keep hammering away at a nation. They will try many tactics . . . infiltration, terrorism, propaganda, attack on the government, weakening the economy, racial strife, and civil unrest.

Communists work hard to sway and change world opinion, so the world will view the Communists as fighting for the workers, fighting for the minorities, fighting to better those under imperialism and capitalism—namely the United States. One has only to look at the people risking their lives to escape from behind the Iron Curtain, the Berlin Wall, or the slave labor camps to see the life they offer their own people.

Soviet propaganda portrays Communists as "peace loving"—not as aggressors working to take over countries such as Afghanistan, South Africa and Mexico. Already many nations like Ethiopia—whose Christian leader, Haile Selassie, mysteriously disappeared—have been overturned and are under Communist rule. Brutality and famine have taken the lives of thousands of people who are not allowed to leave the drought-stricken area. Eventually these "peace loving" Communists plan to defeat America and take over the world.

The World War I hero, Alvin York, said in 1941: The thing people forget is that freedom is so precious we don't just fight for it once and stop."

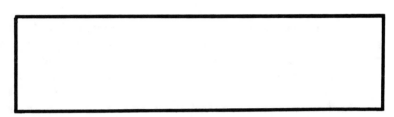

"There will be electrifying, unheard of concessions, *overtures of peace* and capitalists, stupid and decadent, will leap at another opportunity for peace. And when their guard is down—we will smash them—with our clenched fists."

Lenin

Chapter 3

America's Christian Heritage

America's current writers of history textbooks have tried to deny or obscure the fact that our nation was founded upon belief in God. More than that, our forefathers came with a zeal to further the gospel of Jesus Christ in this new undeveloped land.

The faith of the founders of this great nation is very evident in the historical statements which have been documented. The founders never intended a separation of *God* and *State*.

The quotations listed below have been preserved for us and all future generations in scrolls of parchment, on walls and cornerstones of America's historic buildings, on the Liberty Bell, on our coins, and the pages of many books.

These statements reveal their deep faith in God, and an acknowledgement of a total dependency on His divine grace and help to establish this new nation.

It is the responsibility of Christians in America to spread and pass on these *truths* of our Christian heritage to as many people as possible, in order to promote and restore a zeal for righteousness and godliness in our land.

1606—First Charter of Virginia
This charter specified that the Virginia Colony should bring glory to almighty God and advance the Christian faith.

1620—Mayflower Compact

Forty-one Pilgrims prepared the first written constitution of our land. It began: "In the name of God, Amen. Having undertaken for the Glory of God and advancement of the Christian faith . . . do . . . solemnly and mutually in the presence of God covenant and combine ourselves together . . ."

1620—New England Charter

". . . to advance the enlargement of Christian religion, to the glory of God Almighty."

1622—The Carolinas' Charter

Acknowledged that the settlement was constituted for "the propagation of the Christian faith."

1638—Fundamental Orders of Connecticut

". . . confederation together to maintain and preserve the liberty and purity of the gospel of our Lord Jesus which we now profess."

1643—Constitution of the New England Confederation

"Whereas we all came into these parts of America with one and the same end and aim, namely to advance the kingdom of our Lord Jesus Christ and to enjoy the Liberties of the Gospel in purity with peace."

1681—William Penn (Founder of Pennsylvania, Crusader for religious freedom)

"If you are not governed by God, you will be ruled by tyrants."

1752—Liberty Bell

"Proclaim Liberty throughout the land unto all the inhabitants thereof."   Leviticus 25:10.

1772—Samuel Adams (Patriot, Statesman)

"The rights of the Colonists as Christians . . . may be

best understood by reading and carefully studying the insti-
tution of the great Law Giver and Head of the Christian
Church, which are to be found clearly written and promul-
gated in the New Testament."

1775—The Continental Congress
This body officially called all citizens to fast and pray
and confess their sin that God might bless them.

1775—Washington's Cruisers Flag
The flag carries these words: "An Appeal to Heaven"

1776—Declaration of Independence
Four specific references to the dependence of our nation
upon God:
" . . . the laws of Nature and of Nature's God . . ."
". . . that all men are created equal, that they are
endowed by their Creator with certain inalienable rights
. . ."
". . . appealing to the Supreme Judge of the world for
the rectitude of our intentions . . ."
". . . with a firm reliance on the protection of divine
Providence . . ."

1776—Chaplains in the Armed Forces
After signing the Declaration of Independence, General
George Washington issued an order placing a chaplain in
each regiment. They were instructed to have prayers of
thanksgiving to Almighty God.

1787—Benjamin Franklin (Statesman, Diplomat, Scientist,
Inventor)
Franklin helped draft the Declaration of Independence
and was the only man who signed all four of the following
documents: The Declaration of Independence, the Treaty of
Alliance with France, the Treaty of Paris ending the Revolution, and the Constitution.

"Here is my creed. I believe in one God, the creator of the Universe. That he governs it by his Providence. That he ought to be worshipped."

At the Constitutional Convention: "I have lived, Sir, a long time, and the longer I live, the more convincing proofs I see of this truth . . . that God governs in the affairs of men. And if a sparrow cannot fall to the ground without His notice, is it probable that an empire can rise without this aid?" Franklin went on to call for prayer at the beginning of each session.

1787—Alexander Hamilton (America's 1st Secretary of the Treasury)
Soon after the Constitutional Convention: "For my own part, I sincerely esteem it a system which without the finger of God, never could have been suggested and agreed upon by such a diversity of interests."

1789—George Washington—Thanksgiving Day Proclamation
"Whereas it is the duty of all nations to acknowledge the providence of Almighty God, to obey His will, to be grateful for His benefits, and humbly to implore His protection, aid and favors . . . Now, therefore, do I assign and recommend Thursday, the 26th day of November next . . . that we may then all unite in rendering unto Him our sincere and humble thanks for His kind care and protection of the people of this country, and for all the great and various favors which He has been pleased to confer upon us."

1789—George Washington—The Inaugural Address (America's 1st President)
Every President since Washington has included in his inaugural address reference to his and the nation's dependence upon God.

1820—Daniel Webster

(Plymouth, Mass.) ". . . More than all, a government and a country were to commence, with the very first foundations laid under the divine light of the Christian religion . . . Who would wish that his country's existence had otherwise begun?"

"Let us not forget the religious character of our origin."

July 4, 1821—John Quincy Adams (America's 6th President)

"From the day of the Declaration . . . they (the American people) were bound by the laws of God, which they all, and by the laws of the Gospel, which they nearly all, acknowledged as the rules of their conduct."

1861—Abraham Lincoln (America's 16th President)

Farewell words in Springfield, Illinois, February 11: "Unless the great God who assisted him (Washington) shall be with me and aid me, I must fail; but if the same omniscient mind and almighty arm that directed and protected him shall guide and support me, I shall not fail—I shall succeed. Let us all pray that the God of our fathers may not forsake us now."

1863—Abraham Lincoln—The Gettysburg Address

". . . that this nation, under God, shall have a new birth of freedom and that government of the people, by the people, and for the people shall not perish from the earth."

1863—Abraham Lincoln—National Day of Fasting and Prayer Proclamation

". . . it is the duty of nations, as well as of men, to owe their dependence upon the overruling power of God, to confess their sins and transgressions, in humble sorry, yet with assured hope that genuine repentance will lead to mercy and pardon, and to recognize the sublime truth, announced in the Holy Scriptures and proven by all history, that *those nations only are blessed whose God is the Lord* . . ."

". . . We have been the recipients of the choicest bounties of Heaven. We have been preserved these many years in peace and prosperity. We have grown in numbers, wealth, and power as no other nation has ever grown. But we have forgotten God . . . Intoxicated with unbroken success, we have become . . . too proud to pray to the God that made us!"

". . . I hereby request all the People to abstain on that day from their ordinary secular pursuits, and to unite, at their several places of public worship and in their respective homes, in keeping the day holy to the Lord . . .

"All this being done, in sincerity and truth, let us then rest humbly in the hope, authorized by the Divine teachings, that the united cry of the Nation will be heard on high, and answered with blessings, no less than the pardon of our national sins . . ."

1863—Motto On Coins
Secretary of the Treasury, Salmon P. Chase instructed the U.S. mint to begin inscribing "In God We Trust" on all coins.

1892—U.S. Supreme Court
Supreme Court Justice Brewer, delivering the opinion of the Court stated: "These, and many other matters which might be noticed, add a volume of unofficial declarations to the mass of organic utterances—that this is a Christian nation."

July 4, 1913—Woodrow Wilson (America's 28th President)
"Here is the nation God has builded by our hands."

March 3, 1931—National Anthem Adopted by Congress
The Star Spangled Banner closes: "Praise the Power that hath made and preserved us a nation. Then conquer we must, when our cause it is just. And this be our motto—'In God is our Trust'."

June 14, 1954—Pledge of Allegiance

Words "under God" adopted by Congress. "I pledge allegiance to the flag of the United States of America, and to the Republic for which it stands, one nation, under God, indivisible, with liberty and justice for all."

June 20, 1956—National Motto

A joint Resolution was passed by Congress, establishing "In God We Trust" as the national motto of the United States of America.

Other historical declarations of faith:

The Prayer Room in the U.S. Capital Building: located under the rotunda for use by those serving in Congress. A large open Bible lies on the altar facing a stained glass window showing George Washington in prayer.

Jefferson Memorial, Washington, D.C.: Inscribed on the wall is Thomas Jefferson's warning: "God who gave us life gave us liberty. Can the liberties of a nation be secure when we have removed a conviction that these liberties are the gift of God?"

All 50 State Constitutions: All contain a statement of faith recognizing dependence upon Almighty God. Together they become the expression of faith of the American people.

Share these truths at every opportunity.

Chapter 4

America's Christian Textbooks

William H. McGuffey was an American educator and Presbyterian minister. He was a professor at Miami Univeristy in Ohio, and President of Ohio University from 1839-1843. After 1845, he taught moral philosophy at the University of Virginia. William McGuffey is best known for his simple readers which taught children to respect the United States government, and played an important part in forming the moral ideas and literary tastes of Americans in the 1800's.

From 1836 to 1857, Truman and Smith publishers produced his illustrated reading books for the six grades of elementary schools. His readers were approved by Congress for use in the public schools, yet the stories and lessons were often taken directly from the Bible. Congress saw nothing wrong in religious values being taught in America's public schools.

McGuffey's Eclectic Readers were used in all parts of the United States and for many years nearly all American school children learned to read from them. More than 120 million copies were sold during the 1800's.

From Lesson XI of McGuffey's Eclectic Primer for Young Children, designed to precede the Readers, they learned about good and bad behavior, and about God:

"My son, do no bad act.
Go not in the way of bad boys.
A bad boy has woes. He can have no joy.
If you tell a lie, you will be a bad boy.
If you do ill, few will care for you.
If you do well, all will love you.
To have the love of all will give you joy.
If you can not love, you must not hate.
Do not try to hurt him who is a foe,
For God can do to him as He will.
Let it be your joy to do the will of God,
For He can see you, and all you do."

The children learned 26 words and how to spell them. What a difference from "See Dick. See Jane."

From the same Primer, Lesson XIII, a brief story entitled, "The Sick Little Girl," a valuable lesson for everyone:

"Do you see that little girl?
Yes, I see her. She is sick in bed.
Her mother is by her side.
She can not help her.
Can you help the little girl?
No! No one can help her but God.
You may get sick, and I may get sick.
We must ask God to help us when we are sick."

The First Reader, Lesson XX, entitled "John Jones," gives some good advice.

"John Jones was a good boy, but he could not read nor write. His mother was poor. She could not pay for him to go to school. She sent him out to help a man at the side of the road to break stones. John could not earn much, it is true, yet it was good for him to be at work.

"It is well for us all to have work to do. It is bad for us not to work. John was a good boy, and he did not love to play so much that he could not work. He knew it to be right to work, and when his work was done he would play.

"The man for whom John worked was very kind to John, and gave him a great deal of good advice.

"One day he said to him, "John, you must always bear in mind, that it was God who made you, and who gave you all that you have, and all that you hope for. He gave you life, and food, and a home.

"All who take care of you and help you were sent you by God. He sent His Son to show you His will, and to die for your sake.

"He gave you His word to let you know what He hath done for you, and what He wants you to do.

"Be sure that He sees you in the dark, as well as in the day light. He can tell all that you do, and all that you say, and all that is in your mind.

"Oh, ever seek this God!

"Pray to Him when you rise, and when you lie down. Keep His day, hear His word, and do His will, and He will love you, and will be your God forever."

McGuffey's Readers were surely different—they were Christian!

From the First Reader, Lesson XXXI, entitled "Good Advice", teaches forgiveness:

"If you have done anything during the day that is wrong, ask forgiveness of God and your parents.

Remember that you should learn some good things every day. If you have learned nothing all day, that day is lost.

If anyone has done you wrong, forgive him in your heart before you go to sleep. Do not go to sleep with

with hatred in your heart toward anyone.

Never speak to anyone in an angry or harsh voice.

If you have spoken unkind words to a brother or sister, go and ask forgiveness.

If you have disobeyed your parents, go and confess it.

Ask God to aid you always to do good and avoid evil."

Wouldn't it be wonderful to see teaching of character traits like this restored to our public schools?

McGuffey's Spelling Book contained not only spelling, but how the words were to be pronounced and lessons on grammar and punctuation. McGuffey's instructions to assist the teacher were found in the back of the book:

> Let the teacher attend closely to the reading on one of his classes, and he will find "constitution" almost invariably pronounced "const'ution" . . . these defects can only be avoided by great care at a very early stage of the pupil's education. If a faulty articulation becomes fixed while the learner is spelling, it will be almost impossible to correct it entirely . . ."
>
> The advice continued, "Nor should he (student) be permitted to pass over any lesson, until he is able to utter with facility, every sound contained in it, whether vowel or consonant."

The lessons were increasingly difficult and challenging to the students, The Second Reader, Lesson XLIV, told the creation story, "How The World Was Made":

1. When we look on the pleasant earth, we see the green grass and the beautiful flowers. We look around us and see the tall trees and the lofty hills. Between them rolls the bright river, and down their sides flow the clear streams.

2. If we raise our eyes when the sky is clear, we look through the light thin air away to where the bright sun is placed, that shines down upon our world

to give it light and to make it pleasant.

3. These things were not always so. Six thousand years ago there was no pleasant earth, and then the bright sun was not made. The Great God lived then, and there never was a time when He did not live.

4. When the time came that the Creator was pleased to make this world, He made it all out of nothing. When our world was first created, it had nothing beautiful upon it. It was all dark and empty. When God wanted light, He said, "Let there be light, and there was light." God made the air that spreads all around our earth. He made the grass to grow, the lovely flowers, the useful herbs, and all the trees that bear the delicious fruit.

5. After all these things were made, the earth was silent as the grave. There were no cattle to eat the grass, or birds, or the smallest insect to fly through the air. When the fourth day came, He made the glorious sun to shine by day, and the moon and stars to give light by night. When the fourth day ended, the sun set upon a silent world. When the fair moon rose and the stars shone in the sky, there was not a man living on all the earth to behold them.

6. The next day came, and the waters brought forth fish, the birds flew through the soft air, and sang among the trees. On the sixth day, God created the beasts of the field. Last of all, He made man in His own image, and breathed into him the breath of life, and man became a living soul."

Imagine Congress approving that today? The National Education Association and American Civil Liberties Union would have a fit!

At the end of each lesson were questions which had to be answered by the students. These were the thought provoking questions from Lesson XLIV:

1. What do we see as we look around us? 2. Were

these always so? 3. How long is it since the earth was made? 4. By whom was the earth made? 5. What was made on the fourth day? 6. What on the fifth? 7. What on the sixth? 8. What was last made? 9. What is the nobler part of creation? 10. Why is man more noble than the animals and birds? 11. For what should man use these powers?

In 1836, the Second Reader, Lesson LXXXIII, entitled "The Ten Commandments," began:

"1. Every little boy and girl should know the Ten Commandments and be careful to obey them.

2. They were written by God himself, on two tables of stone. He then gave the tables to His servant Moses while he was upon Mount Sinai, amid thunders and lightnings and smoke.

3. The Ten Commandments embrace our duty to God and our neighbors. These are called the law of God.

4. All sin consists in breaking this law. Unfortunately we have all broken it, and have thus become exposed to the penalty, which says, "The soul that sinneth, it shall die."

5. But there is a way of escape from the punishment which we all deserve. The Savior has died and suffered for us. He is able and willing to save all who will seek the forgiveness of God through Him."

There followed a word for word Biblical quotation of the Ten Commandments and ten questions for the students to answer.

McGuffey's NEW Second Reader, Lesson LXII, was a poem entitled, "The Lord's prayer".

"1. Our Father in heaven,
   We hallow thy name!

May thy kingdom holy
On earth be the same!

O, give to us daily
Our portion of bread,

It is from thy bounty
That all must be fed.

2. Forgive our transgressions,
And teach us to know,

That humble compassion,
That pardons each foe;

Keep us from temptation,
From weakness and sin,

And thine be the glory,
Forever: Amen!

By 1865, McGuffey's NEW Second Reader Lesson LXXI, was entitled "The Ten Commandments in Verse". We wonder if there was pressure to omit Bible quotations?

1. Thou no gods shall have but me.
2. Before no idol bend the knee.
3. Take not the name of God in vain.
4. Dare not the Sabbath day profane.
5. Give to thy parents honor due.
6. Take heed that thou no murder do.
7. Abstain from words and deeds unclean.
8. Steal not, for thou by God art seen.
9. Tell not a willful lie, nor love it.
10. What is thy neighbor's do not covet.

The poem ended with these lines:

"With all thy soul love God above;
and as thyself thy neighbor love."

The Supreme Court has ruled that the Ten Commandments cannot be **displayed** in America's public schools, and certainly not taught. It would be wonderful if parents would copy this lesson and ask the teacher to display it as an "Historical document or quotation".

This is how **America**'s public schools began—with Christian textbooks and Biblical morality taught as part of the lessons.

Instead of character traits of honesty, truthfulness, hard work, respect of parents and patriotism, today's students are being taught that it's okay to cheat, lie, steal, and have sex outside of marriage. They call it "Values Clarification" but what it really means is "Destroy Biblical Values" in the lives of the students.

In the classroom, students must make choices and decisions, without discussing it with parents, on such issues as: incest, murder, homosexuality, abortion, lesbianism, and death of the elderly.

One frequently used theme is the lifeboat situation, where there isn't enough room for everyone. The student must decide who gets left on the sinking ship. They learn that the elderly passenger is the obvious choice. In other examples:

1. A student must choose, yet he doesn't know the consequences.

2. A student declares his choice to the class and gives his reasons.

3. A student acts on choice through role-playing in class. An example would be to have a boy argue with a girl about having sex on a date . . . while the class snickers and snorts if morality is mentioned.

The result: to socialize and communize America's children. To make it complete, respect for the Bible must be destroyed.

WHAT HAPPENED TO AMERICA'S SCHOOLS?

A guest on Marlin Maddox's show, *Point of View*, in January 1986, reported certain public schools, specifically one in Illinois, where the children had to **pledge allegience to the Soviet flag** every morning! The students studied **Communist** doctrine and it was extolled . . . all of this as part of a *cultural enrichment program* for the brighter student!

Folks, our tax dollars are paying for this . . . and no one knows about it! Who gives permission for this to be done? Is it the government (Department of Education) or is it a local school board, or just a teacher? We MUST get to the bottom of this and stop it . . . while we can!

Many professors on university staffs in America are sympathetic and supportive of Communist ideology. Gullible students soak up the views of these experts (so-called), and often without question accept their doctrine. If a student does not agree with the Communist philosophy he is ridiculed as not being broad minded or open.

J. Edgar Hoover said, "You, the college student, whether or not you realize it, are the rich earth which the Communist conspirator hopes to till. Your mind is the soil in which he hopes to implant alien seed. Your subsequent acts are the products whose growth he strives to direct. The harvest which he seeks is the destruction of our democratic processes of government."[1]

Hoover stated that the Communist Party had "launched an all-out campaign designed to lure youth into the web of communism . . . by having more national party leaders appear before various student groups at various universities. The Party welcomes opportunities to speak to student groups because it gives the Party an aura of respectability; an opportunity to plant seeds of dissent . . . and an opportunity to recruit some youthful followers."[2]

Hoover said that many college students attended Communist meetings and took part in activities just to prove they weren't closed-minded to Soviet ideology. Some of these students end up teaching in our schools—is it any

wonder that Communists have been so successful in removing God from America's classrooms?

The rapidly growing student New Left movement has
at its core the Students for a Democratic Society, SDS,
which spearheaded the assault in 1968 against Columbia
Unviersity. Students occupied buildings, kidnapped university personnel and deliberately destroyed property. Like the
Communists, they denounce American "capitalism" and
"imperialism"—Marxist words and concepts. The SDS de-
tests the "Establishment"—the military, law enforcement,
and government.

At the SDS Convention in Michigan, June 1968, the New
Leftists waved two flags—the red flag of Socialist communism and the black flag of anarchism. At this "student" convention a workshop on **sabotage and explosives** was held,
including instructions (with illustrations) on how to prepare a
Molotov cocktail and an incendiary time bomb.[3]

If God can't be brought into the classrooms of America's
public schools, we must not allow the religion of godless,
atheistic Communism to be presented.

Chapter 5

Communist Influence In Public Schools

The July 28, 1985, issue of USA TODAY carried a brief report on public education, It stated: "Baltimore, Maryland— Public school system would be ordered not to hire teachers who fail a simple writing test under a new resolution before the City Council. *Of 158 teachers hired this month, 32 failed test. . . .*"

There is talk in many states of testing all teachers, even those who are already on staff in public schools, for their competence in reading and writing. The National Education Association (NEA) is loudly protesting the questioning and testing of their members. But is it unfair to expect and require such competence?

The decision was made by the Oklahoma courts that homosexual teachers could not be fired, nor could schools refuse to hire known homosexuals. This sinful lifestyle is explained as *normal* in many of America's classrooms. "Health" textbooks used in the state of Maryland teach children that **sex with animals is NORMAL** for farm children! And that **homosexuality/lesbianism is NORMAL.**[1] Concerned Women for America newsletter in 1985 reported that the National Education Association was pushing for textbooks that would teach these practices as acceptable and *normal*.

Let's consider what was required of America's early public school teachers. If these rules still applied today there would be few applicants for this noble profession.

RULES FOR TEACHERS—1915

- Must wash the floors once a week with hot soapy water.
- Must build the fire by 7 a.m. so it will be warm for the beginning 8 a.m. school classes.
- Must wear two petticoats.
- Dress must be no more than 2 inches above the ankle.
- Cannot wear any bright colors.
- Cannot dye your hair.
- Can't linger in the ice cream parlors.
- Can't travel out of the city without permission of the School Board.
- Can't travel with a man, unless it's your father or brother.
- Must be dedicated and love your calling more than selfish desires.

One can hardly find this kind of dedication in ministers, much less teachers!

PUBLIC SCHOOLS BEGAN WITH RELIGIOUS TRAINING

Prior to the introduction of public education, Americans were able to choose whatever kind of school or education they wanted for their children. Home schooling was common and there were private schools, church schools, academies for college preparation, seminaries, charity schools for the poor, and tutors. In some towns free schools were supported by private philanthropists.

The original common schools, or public schools, were first created in the New England area as a means of teaching the catechism and insuring the passage of Calvinist Puritan religion from one generation to the next. Bible authority, which replaced Papal authority following the Reformation, required a high degree of Biblical literacy. Thus, the common schools of New England, which were supported by local communities came into being. Early Puritan leaders were impressed with the public schools created by Luther and the German rulers as a means of promoting religious doctrine and social order.

All schools were strictly local schools, financed locally and controlled by local committees who chose their own textbooks and teachers and set their own standards. Latin and Greek were required in public grammar schools, as well as Hebrew in the colleges because these were the Bible languages.

Boston was the only American city to have a public school system at the start of the new nation. Massachusetts was the least tolerant of all the English colonies toward heretical teachings expressed publicly. If it were not for religious reasons, Massachusetts might never have enacted school laws. Other colonies did not enact such school laws, seeming to prefer a greater separation between civil government and religion.[2]

The formation of common schools did not preclude creation of private schools. By 1720, Boston had more private schools than public ones, and by the end of the American Revolution, many towns had no common (public) schools at all.

Public schools were not conceived as a means of lifting the masses from illiteracy. There was no compulsory attendance law. Literacy was a requisite for entering public grammar school at the age of seven.

In 1785, the Continental Congress passed land ordinances, which set aside a section of land in each congressional township for the purpose of creating a state fund for education. Many towns took advantage of this school fund and established common schools, which were only partially financed by the state fund. Counties were required to raise matching funds and parents paid tuition. Private schools were also eligible for subsidies, and most parents preferred them to the public ones.[3]

Public education was not mentioned in the Constitution of the United States and the system we have today did not exist in America until the 1840's. The idea of a state supported and controlled education system, with compulsory attendance, was adopted from Prussia—it did not originate in America.

SOCIALISM IN USA BEGAN AS AN EDUCATIONAL MOVEMENT

Harvard College was founded in 1636, as a seminary for educating the Commonwealth's future leaders as clergymen and magistrates.

In 1805, Harvard became anti-Calvinistic, the citadel of religious and moral liberalism, under the influence of Unitarians. Evil, they believed, is caused by ignorance, poverty, and social injustice. Education would eliminate ignorance, eliminate poverty, eliminate social injustice and crime. Education, they decided, was the only way to solve the problem of evil. Thus the need for the creation of institutions on earth to improve the character of man.[4]

In 1818, in Boston, a city-wide survey of the schooling situation was taken. The first of its kind ever to be made in America revealed that 90 percent of the city's children attended school, without compulsory attendance laws. A vigorous press campaign stressed that the unschooled children must be rescued from neglect or they would become tomorrow's criminals. The persistent campaign for expansion of the public school system paid off.

In 1813, a man in Scotland named Robert Owen began publishing his idea that he had discovered the basic principle of moral improvement. We know him today as the **Father of Socialism**. In 1816, Owen published a plan for a national system of education in England, whereby the character of a whole nation could be molded. Thus, **socialism began as an educational movement**.[5]

In 1917, Lenin said: ". . . Socialism is bound sooner or

later to ripen into Communism, whose banner bears the motto: 'From each according to his ability, to each according to his needs.' "

REMOVING RELIGION FROM PUBLIC SCHOOLS

In those early days, two major issues faced educators: government schools versus private schools, and religious versus secular education.

Edward Hitchcock, in 1845, when extolling the virtues of private schools wrote: ". . . the education of the people is almost entirely under the control of the government . . . a tremendous power for the support of the government, even in a country where the schools are so admirable as in Prussia. But in this country the government presumes that every parent is intelligent and judicious enough to judge what sort of an education is best for his children . . ."[6]

He concluded, "The few among us who are decidedly hostile to religion, can, if they please, attempt to found literary institutions where religion is excluded."[7]

America was largely a religious country and public education would have never gained acceptance if religion had been excluded from it. Orthodox protestants were wary of what secular education would do to the religious faith of American children. Protestant educators and leaders assumed that some religious instruction was not only desirable, but necessary in the public schools, but agreed that it ought not to include doctrines of any particular sect or denomination.

Catholics decided to create a parochial school system in order to preserve the faith of Catholic children, and tried to get public funding for their own schools because of taxation. In the 1850's a report said, ". . . the faith of our children is gradually undermined, and they are trained up to be ashamed of, and to abandon the religion of their fathers. It was bad enough, if this was all done with the money of others; but when it is accomplished, at least in part, *by our own money*, it is really atrocious."

The report continued, ". . . the so-called literature . . .

fostered by our Common Schools, and which is constantly brought to bear on the training of our children, is NOT of a character to form their tender minds to wholesome moral principles, much less to solid Christian piety . . . it is pagan."[8]

Immoral literature, fostered in public schools, was infecting the minds of America's children in 1850—how much worse it is in 1986!

In 1840, Bishop Hughes told New York City officials: **to make an infidel what is necessary to do? Cage him up in a room, give him a secular education from the age of five years to twenty-one**, and I ask you what he will come out, if not an infidel? . . . was it the intention of the Legislature of New York . . . that the public schools should be made precisely such as the infidels want?[9]

The Catholic issue had settled the matter of public funding—only secular public schools would be the beneficiaries of public funds. A truly neutral government would have agreed to fund **all** schools, religious or otherwise.

By 1905, 22 percent of all public expenditures in the United States would be spent on public education.[10]

In 1965, passage of the Elementary and Secondary Education Act of 1965 opened the floodgate of federal money to public education.

Written into the act were "specific prohibitions against the allocation of any funds by the states . . . for direct support of private or parochial schools and the use of any of the money from the act to finance or enhance or to promote in any religious instruction."[11]

The *Muskegon Chronicle*, April 6, 1985, reported that atheist leader Madalyn Murry O'Hair said her organization would push for **atheist training** in the nation's public schools, calling religious philosophy the dregs of human thought.

Since the enactment of the Elementary and Secondary Education Act of 1965, more than *$42 billion* of America's wealth has been pumped into the public schools. The NEA has frequently repeated one quotation from the National Commission on Excellence in Education's 1983 report. It is: "Excellence costs. But in the long run mediocrity costs far more." In other words, give NEA more money and they'll provide the quality that has eluded the schools all these years.

Is money the answer?

The cost of public elementary and secondary education is staggering:

> In 1960, America funded $15.6 billion.
> In 1970, it rose to $40.6 billion.
> In 1983, it had increased 800 percent over 1960, to a cost of $141.0 billion dollars.

In addition, Congress had enacted over 100 federal programs aiding education.[12]

The National Education Association hopes that president Lyndon B. Johnson was correct in his statement that "once started, federal aid to education will never be stopped."

Yet, with all this generous funding to education, the reading scores have declined alarmingly since 1965. *Education Week* reported on May 16, 1984, "student scores have dropped on standardized reading tests in two of the nation's largest public-school populations—California and New York . . ."[13]

The *Dallas Morning News* carried an interesting article entitled "Young People Are Getting Dumber." The director of Human Engineering Laboratory, which specializes in aptitude testing, said: "Do you know that all laboratories around the country are recognizing *a drop in vocabulary of one percent a year*? In all our 50 years of testing it's never happened before. **Can you imagine what a drop in knowledge of 1 percent a year for 30 years could do to our civilization?"**

The decline in intellectual and academic skills of American students is what has brought us to this dangerous state of affairs. The emphasis in public schools on sex education, values clarification, sensitivity training, role playing, group activities, and other teachings will never make up for the deficiency in academic training.

There seems to be only one way out for the American people—a mass exodus from the public schools into private ones, where a strong academic foundation is still possible.

THE ECLECTIC SERIES.   21

LESSON IV.

blest	guide	tar'dy	teach'er
learn	wrong	les'sons	school'-boy
haste	i'dler	end'less	knowl'edge

Chapter 6

Phonics and Communism

In 1910, statistics compiled by the Bureau of Education indicated that only 22 out of every 1,000 children, from 10-14 years of age, could neither read nor write. Ten states: Connecticut, District of Columbia, Massachusetts, Minnesota, Montana, New Hampshire, North Dakota, Oregon, Utah, and Washington, reported that only 1 child in 1,000 between 10 and 14 was illiterate.[1]

Apparently the public school teachers knew how to teach children to read in 1910, for there were no functional illiterates or "reading disabled" children. The illiteracy of 1910 was the result of some children having no schooling. Children in school learned to read, including the not-so-bright, and culturally disadvantaged minorities. Dyslexia was so rare that most people had never even heard of it.

The January, 1915 issue of *School and Society* quoted U.S. Bureau of Education, "It is evident that the public schools will in a short time practically eliminate illiteracy."[2]

A short time? In the succeeding seventy years, it hasn't worked that way. Why? It's something that has mystified Americans.

The government spends more money on education than ever before, yet the Department of Education estimates that there are **24 million** functional illiterates in the United States, virtually all of whom have had from eight to twelve years of compulsory public schooling![3]

What has caused this decline in reading and writing skills

in America? For many concerned parents, the decline can be traced back to the 1930's when public schools discarded the phonics method of teaching children to read.

In 1896, one of America's educational leaders, John Dewey, wrote: "It is one of the **great mistakes** of education to make reading and writing constitute the bulk of the school work the first two years. The true way is to teach them *incidentally* as the outgrowth of the social activities at this time . . ."[4]

Dewey's LOOK-SAY METHOD of teaching reading was not put into practice in the classrooms of America quickly. Textbooks had to be written, and teachers trained. The new methods were slipped into the schools because the American people were never informed of what was taking place nor given a choice.

In 1908, G. Stanley Hall went so far as to **extol the virtues of illiteracy**! He wrote: ". . . illiterates . . . escape much eyestrain and mental excitement . . . lead a useful, happy, virtuous life . . . escape certain temptations, such as vacuous and vicious reading . . ."[5]

That same year Hall wrote, ". . . instead of taking half the time of the first year or two of school to teach reading, *little attention should be paid to it before the beginning of the third year* . . . there should be NO reading for the sake of reading, for this is never an end . . ."

Dr. Samuel T. Orton, a professor of psychiatry at Iowa State University, who specialized in speech disorder, wrote an article entitled "The Sight-Reading Method of Teaching Reading," published in the February, 1929, issue of the *Journal of Educational Psychology*. Orton wrote: "I wish to emphasize . . . that the sight method of teaching reading . . . often proves an actual *obstacle to reading* progress!"

Dr. Orton's article continued: "and moreover I believe that . . . faulty teaching methods may not only prevent the acquisition of academic education by children of average capacity but *may also give rise to far reaching damage to their emotional life*."[6]

John Dewey first formulated the notion that **high liter-**

acy is an obstacle to socialism. High literacy gave the individual the means to seek knowledge independently . . . a detriment to building a socialist society.

We must remember what Lenin said about Socialism: *"Socialism is bound sooner or later to ripen into communism."*

In 1936, authors of *The Dewey School* wrote of his Laboratory School: ". . . undue premium is put upon the ability to learn to read at a certain chronological age . . ."[7]

Dewey's views were concealed in his writing style, described by Max Eastman as "dynamite . . . in a pile of dry hay". Take, for example, a line Dewey wrote in 1935 in "Liberalism and Social Action": "The last stand of oligarchical and anti-social seclusion is perpetuation of this purely individualistic notion of intelligence."[8]

His goal apparently was to produce inferior readers with inferior intelligence, dependent on a social education elite for guidance and wisdom. It's been successfully carried out in America's public schools!

SOVIET CONNECTION

Dr. W. Horsley Gantt, of Johns Hopkins University spent five years, from 1922 to 1929, working in Russian laboratories, when **the Soviets experimented with methods of artificially inducing behaviorial disorganization in humans**. Dr. Gantt translated into English a book by Soviet psychologist Aleksandr R. Luria, which was published in 1932 in the United States. Dr. Luria's experiments indicate that *psychologists knew how to* **artificially** *induce dyslexic behavior.*[9]

Reading problems, caused by the look-say reading method adopted by America's public schools, were blamed on dyslexia. Yet dyslexia was almost unheard of before 1930.

Students taught to read by the phonics method did not experience the confusing symptoms of dyslexia.

In 1925, the Soviet government established a Bureau of Cultural Relations between the U.S.S.R. and Foreign Countries, which in 1927 set up a subsidiary in the United States— The *American Society for Cultural Relations with Russia* (ASCRR).

John Dewey and Stephen P. Duggan were Vice Presidents, and William Allen Neilson of Smith College was President.

The main work of the American Society For Cultural Relations With Russia was to facilitate the exchange of students, professors and scientists between the two countries.[10]

By the 1930's, American and Soviet psychologists and psychiatrists had an intimate working relationship. In 1930, Dr. Gantt established the Pavlovian Laboratory at the Phibbs Psychiatric Clinic at Johns Hopkins University.

According to the *New York Times*, Stephen L. Duggan, was director of the Institute of International Education, which sponsored Moscow summer schools which got underway in 1934. Duggan wrote: "In the fall of 1933 I was invited by the Soviet Government to go to Moscow to advise with it as to the best methods to develop cultural relations between the United States and the Soviet Union . . . ."

Duggan concluded: "I invited a number of distinguished educators to form an advisory council. Everyone invited accepted the invitation . . . ."

On July 23, 1934, the *New York Times* reported that Americans of many types, ranging from members of students' radical oganizations to Groton graduates planning to enter Harvard or Yale that fall, were among a group of about 200 Americans who attended the Anglo-American Institute of Moscow University, where they were offered a variety of courses in education. Courses were in psychology, economics, and sociology, all were taught in English by Soviet professors.

One of the courses taken by the Americans was called "Psycho-politics." According to K.M. Heaton, it was "the application of psychology and principles of mental health . . . , **to the conquest of the United States by the Communists.**"[10]

It hardly seems possible that our own citizens and educators were actually studying how to overthrow and defeat America, but history indicates they did.

The Moscow summer school of 1935 was promoted by a full page ad in the *NEA Journal*.

The school was abruptly cancelled after about 200 Americans had arrived in Moscow, evidently due to Stalin's massive purge of the Communist party.

Laurence Duggan, son of Stephen P. Duggan, succeeded his father as director of the Institute of International Education, and was implicated by Whittaker Chambers as belonging to a Communist spy ring. Laurence had been interviewed by the FBI and was scheduled to testify before a Congressional committee investigating the *infiltration of the U.S. government by Communist agents,* when he fell, jumped, or was pushed to his death from a window of his sixteenth floor office in New York.[11]

HONESTY IN TEXTBOOKS

There seems to be a lack of honesty in America's textbooks. At a White House briefing in November, 1985, Gary Bower reported on education in public schools. He pointed out some issues we need to be aware of:

1. In 1984, a teacher from Arlington, Virginia reported that 51 out of 53 students could see *no difference* between Communism and the U.S.A.

2. A textbook used in history and civics classes, published by Harper and Row, *Human Expression, A History of the World*, gives a highly favorable view of the USSR. It pointed out that they have "Equal Pay" for women (the government sets the wages which are very low). Women can vote at 18 (but only one candidate to choose from). The book has 854 pages and covers suffering of a famine in the 1930's, but has no mention of the millions who died in Cambodia, Hungary, and Afghanistan because of USSR genocide.

   When asked why they had eliminated Soviet brutality, the reply was: **"So the children wouldn't be hostile to Communism!"** No honesty in writing.

3. A study for the National Endowment for the Humanities found that *half* of the students surveyed didn't recognize Churchill or Stalin's name! Neither did they know when the Civil War took place, or when the Declaration of Independence was signed. What is being taught in History classes, we wonder?

4. The word "inalienable" has been *omitted* from the Declaration of Independence, in a 7th grade textbook. The reason? The children wouldn't understand the word! This omits God, who gave these rights.

5. The National Council for Social Studies handbook for teachers uses the comparative approach on issues such as: right to take a vacation, the right to vote, right to strike and freedom of speech—claiming these exist in eastern Europe. (Ask Lech Walensa about these freedoms.)

6. Americans need to know what's going on. George Will reported that a 3rd grade teacher in the USSR was killed by a live hand grenade. Combat training is being taught. The Russian children are told that they will have to fight Americans and kill the capitalists . . . and that they must lay down their lives for their homeland. (Our students are playing while Marxists are dismantling rifles, blindfolded!)

Parents need to talk to their children about our history. Tell them what happened at Pearl Harbor and Omaha Beach. Remind them that our liberty was hard won by brave Americans. Arlington Cemetery is visible evidence that our freedoms are not guaranteed.

Abraham Lincoln appreciated America's freedom, he said: "Many free countries have lost their liberties . . . to my country I swear eternal fidelity, my life, my liberty and my love."

Parents have the right and the responsibility to raise their children, and to educate them. Parents should know what is being taught. Ask to read the books and don't let yourself be ignored or set aside.

Perhaps the voucher system being proposed in Congress will provide an answer—by providing limited funds so that parents can choose private or Christian schools instead of public schools. Something must be done. Many of America's Christian parents see the need for a drastic change, or total withdrawal from the atheistic, humanistic public school system.

Chapter 7

Schools—War Is Raging

In 1930, the first edition of the *Dick and Jane* primers, by William Scott Gray, Dean of the University of Chigago's School of Education, were published. They would soon become the dominant reading textbooks in America's primary schools, making millions of dollars for both publisher and author.

Yet, in only five years, after *Dick and Jane* primers had gotten into the schools, Gray wrote an article in the *Elementary English Review* which described many exotic medical conditions which were causing a national epidemic in reading disability, such as: congenital aphasia, dyslexia, developmental alexia, congenital alexia, strephosymbolia, cerebral dominance, emotional instability, defective vision, and mental retardation.[1]

In 1936, the *National Education Association Journal* published a series of articles which pointed out that "there are probably nearly *half a million children in the first four grades of American schools* . . . (with) *serious disabilities in reading.*"

The Great Depression probably kept millions of American children from becoming functional illiterates because many schools could not afford the new look-say textbooks, and continued to use the old phonics books. When these books wore out, schools had no choice. Phonics books were no longer published!

In April 1944, *Life* magazine reported: "Millions of children in the U.S. suffer from dyslexia which is the medical term for reading difficulties. It is responsible for about 70% of the school failures in 6 to 12 year-age-group."

The article went on to say: "Dyslexia may stem from . . . glandular imbalance, heart disease, eye or ear trouble—or deep-seated psychological disturbance that 'blocks' a child's ability to learn."

The report told of a little girl with an I.Q. of 118, being examined at the Dyslexia Institute of Northwestern University. Doctors concluded the girl needed *"thyroid treatments, removal of tonsils and adenoids, and exercises to strengthen her eye muscles."* The *Life* story concluded: "Other patients may need dental work, nose, throat or ear treatments . . . ."[2]

The "blockage" to learning (dyslexia) was never heard of until the introduction of the sight-reading textbooks. Yet Gray, Gates, and other look-say authors denounced any criticism of their methods. The behaviorist educators have always known that artificially induced dyslexia could be *eliminated overnight* by switching grade schools back to phonics.

An editorial in the *Boston Globe* on March 11, 1984 stated that "about 40 percent of the city's adult population is believed to be functionally illiterate." What a difference from 1910 when the U.S. Bureau of Education reported that 1 out of 1,000 children between 10 and 14 in Massachusetts were illiterate.

Despite this evidence, and frantic pleas from parents overwhelmingly in favor of phonics, *most of the schools in America still teach the look-say method*, to the detriment of America's children.

What is the National Education Association's reaction? In their 1983-84 Annual Edition of *Today's Education*, they declared: **"the overemphasis on phonics with beginners is now ready for the scrap heap."**

An article in the *Journal of Reading*, December 1981, entitled "Teaching Reading in the Cuban Primary Schools," tells of education and literacy in Communist Cuba. Teams of curriculum experts in the 1970's chose the Phonic/Analytic/Synthetic method of teaching reading, which was developed in the Soviet Union and still in use there. The article revealed the Soviet method could be traced to the work of Alexander Luria and his associates.

The article tells us: "... for languages which have alphabet writing systems based on phonics (such as Spanish or English), Luria believes that reading should be approached primarily through the auditory channel (phonics)."

"While many children learn to read by the 'sight' approach, they usually do not develop the 'phonematic hearing which . . . *hampered* their development in other language skills of spelling, writing, and speech articulation. To bypass such auditory training is to deprive the child of an important key to language."[3]

The reported concluded: "In the United States, the approach closest to the Soviet Phonic/Analytic/Synthetic Method was developed by the late 1930's by Anna Gillingham, an educator, in collaboration with Samuel Orton, a neurologist interested in dyslexia. Orton decried the use of 'sight' method in the schools and emphasized the importance of the auditory blending . . . termed the 'Orton' approach . . . intensive phonics . . . known to be particularly effective in teaching dyslexic students."

Artificially induced dyslexia is the most common learning disability in the United States today.

Orton's warnings were ignored by American educators. In fact, they actually increased the dosage of look-say. They resisted all pressures to return to intensive phonics.

John Dewey visited Soviet schools in 1928. Professor Counts toured the Soviet Union in 1927 and 1929. During his visits Counts consulted people in charge of Soviet education, including Lenin's widow, N.K. Krupskaya, who wrote in her *Reminiscences of Lenin*, how *phonics was used* to teach illiterate Red Army soldiers to read during their civil war of 1919.[4]

The NEA has established cordial relations with Soviet and Nicaraguan teachers who use *intensive phonics* to teach their children to read. Yet—the *NEA keeps pushing the look-say method of reading on American children!*

The National Commission on Excellence in Education issued a report in April 1983, entitled, *A Nation at Risk*, in which it said: "The educational foundations of our society are presently being eroded by a rising tide of mediocrity that threatens our very future as a nation and as a people."

The report continued, "*If an unfriendly foreign power* had attempted to impose on America the mediocre educational performance that exists today, we might well have viewed it as *an act of war.* As it stands, we have allowed this to happen to ourselves."

Hasn't an *unfriendly foreign power* done just that?

NEA ESTABLISHED

Initially called the National Teachers Association, the organization was founded in Philadelphia in 1857. The aim of the group was "to elevate the character and advance the interests of the profession of teaching, and to promote the cause of public education in the United States."

One of the organizers, Thomas W. Valentine said: "What we want is an association that shall embrace all teachers of our whole country . . . we need not merely to promote the interests of our profession, but to gather up and arrange the educational statistics of our country, so that the people may know what is really being done for public education and what yet remains to be done."

In 1857, membership was open to "any gentleman regularly occupied in teaching—or editor of an educational journal, or a superintendent of schools." Women were admitted to membership in 1866.

In 1870, the name was changed to National Education Association, and membership was opened to "any person in any way connected with the work of education."

In 1984, NEA membership was expanded to include "ALL PERSONS actively engaged in the profession of teaching or in other education work OR to persons interested in advancing the cause of public education . . . ," thus enabling book publishers, salesmen, and suppliers to take advantage of the benefits of the organization.[5]

WAR IS RAGING

The NEA is fighting tooth and nail against teacher competency testing. Where they have been tested, as in Dallas and Houston in 1978, the results have been dismal. Arkansas is one state that has dared mandate testing of its 24,000 teachers to see how well they read, write, and do arithmetic. Teachers who fail must improve their skills or lose certification.

An article in July 28, 1985 issue of *USA Today* indicated a resolution before the Baltimore, Maryland City Council would order the public school system not to hire teachers who failed a simple writing test. Of the 158 teachers hired that month, 32 teachers failed the test!

While the NEA is dead-set against testing the skills of public school teachers, it is pressing for testing to "evaluate" church school teachers; a double standard to be sure. The NEA is pressing for regulation of private schools—it's not a matter of education—it's a matter of money and power.

In 1977, a student in New York state brought suit against his school district for graduating him despite his being functionally illiterate. The Court of Appeals dismissed the case saying: "Recognition in the courts of this cause of action would constitute blatant interference with the responsibility for the administration of the public-school system . . . ."[6]

The courts don't want to interfere with administration of the public-school system, but they seem to forget the right of private religious schools to operate.

Article 1 of the Bill of Rights states: **"Congress shall make no law respecting an establishment of religion, or prohibiting the free exercise thereof."**

That issue was settled in 1925, in a Supreme Court case *Pierce v. Society of Sisters,* when it decided the case in favor of the private parochial school: "since public schools cannot engage in religious instruction, private schools are indispensable to the free exercise of religion."

The recent case in Nebraska showed America that religious freedom is not to be taken lightly. Peter Hoagland,

State Senator from Nebraska, told a television audience on April 15, 1982: "What we are most interested in, of course, are the children themselves . . . we don't think they (Rev. Sileven or parents) should be entitled to *impose decisions or religious philosophies on their children*, which could seriously undermine those children's ability to deal in this complicated world when they grow up."

More and more the war is raging in the courts against religion. In May 1984, the ACLU won a suit to prevent an invocation, benediction, or religious hymn from being included in a high school commencement exercise. The judge, according to *Education Week*, ruled that the *inclusion of a prayer at graduation* is a *violation* of the Constitutional prohibition of official sanction of religious beliefs."

In May 1984, the Michigan Attorney General ruled it was *unconstitutional* for a voluntary 30 minute Bible-study class, which had met once a week for the past 25 years in several public schools in the state, to do so . . . after the ACLU filed a complaint.[7]

Parents are being persecuted, fined, and imprisoned as many states are bearing down on home-schooling, although the children are doing better academically at home than they might have done in school. These parents also feel teaching Biblical morality is vital, but these values would be ridiculed in public schools as outmoded religious doctrine.

In addition to concern for teaching the 3-R's, these parents wish to protect their children from sex education which teaches that premarital sex, abortion, and homosexuality are acceptable freedoms. Soon these "freedoms" could include in-school abortions.

The January 1986 issue of *Intercessors For America Newsletter* carried a report on *school-based sex clinics*. In New York City, the Center for Population Options is operating a support clinic. The reported goal of these clinics is not just to offer sex education and to *openly distribute contraceptives*, but eventually to *administer in-school abortions!* Thirty such clinics *now exist* with plans to open another 35 in 1986!

The United States Supreme Court has ruled that minors

have the right to receive birth control medication and abortion WITHOUT their parents' consent.

The December 1985 *Concerned Women For America Newsletter* discussed a 1985 report, *A Psychoanalytic Look at Today's Sex Education: A Guide for the Perplexed.* The author, Dr. Melvin Anchell, a human sexuality expert, links public sex education programs to rises in teenage pregnancy, suicide, depression, and drug use.

The September/October, 1985 issue of *Family Research Today* carried a report in which Dr. Melvin Anchell pointed out that "Sex education programs from kindergarten through high school CONTINUOUSLY DOWNGRADE the intimate, affectionate, monogamous nature of human sexuality."

Dr. Anchell indicated that exposing 6-to-12 year-old children to sex education programs can:
1. Make the child less educable
2. Block the child's development of compassion
3. Weaken the mental barriers controlling base sexual instincts (thereby making the child vulnerable to perversions in later life).[9]

GOD HELP US ALL

We wonder if President Reagan knows what is really going on in American schools? In his televised pre-summit talk, the President said he hopes two of the ways we can lessen the distrust between our peoples would be:

1. If Soviet youth could attend American schools and learn, first-hand, that a spirit of freedom rules our land, and that we do not wish the Soviet people any harm.

To that idea we would have to reply: that there is no such spirit of freedom in American schools. Like the Soviet schools, the public schools in America have banished God. Like the Soviet schools, these things CANNOT be taught in public schools:
1. The earth was created by God

2. God created heaven
3. God created the sun, moon, and stars
4. God created man—you cannot teach these things.

Nor can our schools teach moral absolutes, such as:
1. Homosexuality is a sin
2. Adultery is a sin
3. Stealing is a sin
4. Abortion is murder.

Nor can our children learn about:
1. Eternal life
2. Heaven
3. Judgment
4. Hell.

However, our public schools declare they have total reading freedom. Freedom to read books filled with four-letter words. Freedom to read anything you want—except the Bible.

If we do not wish any harm to the Soviet people, why suggest sending their children to our public schools? Teachers are unable to discipline cases of assault, extortion, or drug peddling. America's parents are concerned with their children's safety in the public schools.

2. If American youth could do likewise (attend Soviet schools), President Reagan suggests they could talk about their interests and values, and hopes for the future with their Soviet friends. The President noted that in Soviet schools, our children would learn that: "we're all God's children with much in common."

In the Soviet schools, "scientific atheism" is a mandatory subject, and the only mention of God is the denial of His existence. Our children certainly would not learn that "we're all God's children."

If our kids did attend Soviet schools, they could not talk freely about anything, much less about "their interests and values, and hopes for the future."

America has enough educational problems now without the added expense of "exchanging" thousands of our youngsters with Soviet students.

Americans are already paying taxes to have our children brainwashed against God, and increasingly taught to have global patriotism instead of patriotism for our own country. God help us all.

Chapter 8

Schools Teach A New Religion
ATHEISTIC HUMANISM

America is facing a crisis. Humanists have crept into key positions of influence in all forms of government. In many cases, without realizing it, we have voted in officials who have advocated abortion, homosexuality, prostitution, pornography, and removing prayer from the schools.

Humanism as we know it today began with two French skeptics—Voltaire and Rousseau. They propagated antimoral philosophy through their writings. Later, the so-called "Age of Reason" invaded colleges and universities and produced acceptance of Marxism, rationalism, Freudianism, and existentialism.

The Humanist Manifestos I and II both state that Humanism is a religion, a faith.[1]

The Supreme Court, in the 1961 case of *Torcaso v. Watkins*, has declared secular humanism to be a religion equivalent to theistic and other nontheistic religions.

Their "bible"—*The Humanist Manifestos I and II*—reveals the vicious hatred of Christian values, and the existence of a "new faith—a religion of humanity."

Here are some quotes from the *Humanist Manifesto II*, which illustrate their doctrine:

"As in 1933, (the date of the Humanist Manifesto I) *Humanists still believe that* traditional theism, especially *faith in the prayer-hearing God*, assumed to love and care for persons, to hear and understand their prayers, and to be able to do some-

thing about them, *is an unproved and out-moded faith*. Salvation-
ism, based on mere affirmation, still appears as *harmful*, divert-
ing people with false hopes of heaven hereafter. Reasonable
minds look to *other means* for survival."[2]

"We find insufficient evidence for belief in the existence of a supernatural. We begin with humans, not God,
nature, not deity. Traditional religions often offer solace to
humans, but as often, they inhibit humans from helping
themselves or experiencing their full potentialities, often
impede the will to serve others, encourage dependence
rather than independence, obedience rather than affirma-
tions, fear rather than courage. **No deity will save us, we
must save ourselves.**"[3]

"Science affirms that the human species is an emergence
from natural evolutionary forces . . . there is no credible
evidence that life survives the death of the body. Ethics is
autonomous and situational, needing no theological or ideological sanctions."[4]

"In the area of sexuality, we believe that intolerant atti-
tudes often cultivated by orthodox religions and puritanical
cultures, unduly repress sexual conduct."[5]

The *Humanist Manifesto II*, says: "It (the state—or government) should *not* favor *any* particular religious bodies, through
the use of public monies."[6]

Yet, ironically, it is the *Humanist religion* that the United
States courts and government favor above all others.

"We look to the development of a system of world law
and world order based upon *Trans-national federal government*."[7]

"It is the moral obligation of developed nations to provide
through an international authority . . . massive assistance
including birth control techniques. Extreme disproportions in
wealth, income, and economic growth should be reduced on a
worldwide basis."[8]

"Commitment to all humankind is the highest commitment of which we are capable: it transcends the narrow
allegiances of the church, state, party, class or race; each
person to become a citizen of the world community."[9]

BRAINWASHED

Humanism has become rooted in our educational system and is spreading like an infectious disease. The victims are our precious children. Our children are being brainwashed into an acceptance of evolution, atheism, abortion, adultery, homosexuality, immorality, and pornography through the efforts of Humanists in the schools and the media.

Who would think the Humanists would be so bold as to declare their intentions of using the public schools to convert our children to their religion?

This is exactly what they've done in an article by John Dunphy in the January-February, 1983 issue of *Humanist Magazine*. It reads in part:

"I am convinced that the battle for humankind's future must be waged and won in the public school classroom . . . by teachers . . . who correctly perceive their role as *proselytizers of a new faith: a religion of humanity* . . . that recognizes and respects what theologians call *divinity* in every human being."

"These teachers must embody the same selfless dedication as the most rabid fundamentalist preachers, for they will be *ministers of another sort . . . utilizing the classroom instead of a pulpit* . . . to convey the Humanist values in whatever subject they teach . . . *regardless of the educational level*—preschool, day care center, or large state university."

"The classroom *must* and *will* become an arena of conflict between the old and the new—*the rotting corpse of Christianity*, together with all its adjacent evils and misery, and *the new faith of Humanism . . .*"

" . . . *it will undoubtedly be a long, arduous, painful struggle replete with much sorrow and many tears, BUT HUMANISM WILL EMERGE TRIUMPHANT.*"[10]

What can Christians do to combat Humanism?

SOME GUIDELINES

1. Put on the whole armor of God, (Ephesians 6:10-18).

For we are not fighting against human beings, but
demonic unseen forces.

2. Daily speak aloud a prayer of protection and release,
for yourself and your loved ones, such as the one that
Catherine Marshall LeSourd wrote out and referred
to often during the last months of her life:

"Satan, I say to you—in the mighty name of Jesus
Christ—release me and every member of my family
from every hold you ever had on us. In the Name of
Jesus, I take back any territory I may have given you in
my lifetime. In the Name of Jesus I cancel any curse
against me or any member of my family. In the Name
of Jesus, I cut myself free from bondage to any person
living or dead. I claim the protection of the blood of
Jesus over my mind, over my body and over my spirit. I
close the door on you, satan, never to be opened
again!"[11]

3. Repent of watching too much television, and allowing
immoral values to creep into your home through
these programs. (I John 1:9)

4. Don't wink at sin. Be careful what you expose your
eyes to, your ears to. If YOU don't censor the TV
shows your children watch they'll be absorbing witchcraft, sorcery, violence, and occult plots which will
open them to deception and weaken their spiritual life.
Screen out evil, take no part in it, and expose it. (Ephesians 5:11)

5. Vow to fill your mind with uplifting, good things
which reflect your love of the Lord and God's Word
(Philippians 4:8-9). Enjoy family fun. Turn off the TV.
Talk! Read good books. Sing, listen to godly music.
Play games, picnic, hike, or take part in other recrea-
tion with family or friends. Perhaps now is the time to
take lessons and learn to play a musical instrument.

6. Spend time daily in Bible study and prayer (Joshua
1:8). The key to overcoming satanic attacks, problems,
pressures, and worries is giving time to meditate on
God's Word and apply it to your situation. HE has

promised you'll have good success! (Mark 6:31—come to Jesus and rest.)

7. Exercise your will (Romans 12:1-2). Don't follow the crowd. Don't be pressured by worldly friends to "let your hair down" and join them. Be renewed in your *mind*, the gatekeeper of your soul. You alone make the choice. Cooperate with Jesus—remind your children satan works to weaken their will.

8. Be a doer of the Word (James 1:22). Be an example in conversation and actions of godly behavior to your children, neighbors, family, and coworkers. Walk righteously and speak what is right. Speak out against abortion and immorality. Don't just ignore it, expose it! (Ephesians 5:11). Let your children know God's standards are to be praised.

Chapter 9

Communism— A Mortal Challenge

John Noble, who vanished for nine years in a Russian slave camp testified, "We are drowning in a sea of complacency. Americans simply do not want to care. Don't be complacent!"[1]

"Face the facts, no matter how unpleasant. The Communists say this is a fight to the finish. Believe them!" Rev. W.S. Mooneyham, editor of an evangelical magazine, wrote. "Krushchev said, 'We will bury you.' He meant it. Keep your head out of the sand and face the issue squarely."

Do you see the peril that lies at America's doorstep? It is a deadly challenge we cannot ignore. Communism is not just another ideology, but a political system that desires to destroy America. We must face the challenge and meet it, if our freedom is to survive the Communist threat.

An article from *Paix et Liberte*, a French Communist newspaper, reveals their determination and willingness to sacrifice time, money, and even their lives for what they believe:

"We Communists do not play with words. We are realists, and seeing that we are determined to achieve our object, we know how to obtain the means. Of our salaries and wages we keep only what is strictly necessary; and give the rest for propaganda purposes. To this propaganda we also consecrate all our free time and part of our holidays.

"You (Christians) however, give only a little time and hardly any money for the spreading of the gospel of Christ. How can anyone believe in the supreme value of this gospel if you do not practice it, if you do not spread it, and if you sacrifice neither time nor money for it?

"Believe me, it is we who will win, for we believe in our Communist message and are ready to sacrifice everything, even our life, in order that social justice shall triumph. But you people are afraid to soil your hands." [2]

We must not minimize the real danger of Communism.

One of the most important tactics of Communism is *infiltration*—the placing of Communists in non-Communist groups, such as: civic, religious, cultural, and economic groups, as well as labor unions. This is an effective technique in spreading Marxist-Leninist influence and ideas.

"Learn to penetrate into prohibited premises where the representatives of the bourgeoisie exercise influence over the workers" is a dictum of Lenin which is taken most seriously by Communists. They are interested in employment in the most vital industries in America—high technology, automobile, steel, coal, rubber. Once in a vital spot, a Communist can cause great industrial damage to our economy and can help other Communists gain employment.

Communists are trying to join women's community clubs, youth organizations, and political groups. Once "inside" a legitimate organization, they might elect a "favorable" candidate, influence policy or decisions. They misguide many unsuspecting loyal citizens into support of policies fostered by the Communists wherever possible.

In the 1930's, Communism became acceptable in America—just another philosophy. The communists achieved growth through the American Labor Party in New York, the Progressive Federation in Wisconsin, the Farmer-Labor Party in Minnesota, and the Commonwealth Federation in Washington. The Communist party supported the struggle of John L. Lewis and all others in their fight to strengthen the American Federation of Labor unions.[3]

Thousands took their lead from the Communists without affiliating with the party. Somewhere between 200,000 and 250,000 American people joined it during the 1930's. Secret party members held positions of influence in numerous non-Communist organizations.

In 1936, for the first time a Communist candidate spoke to the National Press Club, and received support from the nation's press who defended the Communist Party's RIGHT to campaign without hinderance.

Two Communist congressional candidates were elected in New York in 1936. Audiences around the country were large and enthusiastic. The *Chicago Tribune* published a report that *Moscow had ordered the American Communists to back Franklin D. Roosevelt.*[4]

Norman Thomas campaigned for President of the United States, his slogan: **Socialism versus Capitalism**.

". . . *Socialism is bound sooner or later to ripen into Communism,"* said Lenin in 1917.

In January 1936, Al Smith spoke to a Liberty League Banquet warning: "There can be only one capital, Washington or Moscow."

At a Central Committee meeting held from June 17-20, 1937, the Communists decided to invite themselves into the Democratic party. Rather than expend energy in difficult struggles to overcome legal and political obstacles to a third party, the Communists had a new task. The objective was to encourage *"systematic and organized activity within the Democratic Party,* (in some cases, the Republican Party), making the fullest possible use of the democratic possibilities of the primary election machinery to name decisively anti-fascist and progressive candidates and formulating a clear program of progressive social and labor legislation."[5]

Washington Communists discovered just how open American political parties were. "You are a member of whatever you say you are," Terry Pettus recalled, explaining how a relatively small group of activists could win control of a large segment of the Democratic party. Their avid support for the New Deal enabled them to make startling gains.[6]

Communists became an acceptable ally in all kinds of movements. The Communists supported abolition of Reserve Officer Training Corps (ROTC): "as we fight all moves of American imperialism to build up its war machine."

Beginning in 1933, the Party had carried on a frenzied campaign against the Civilian Conservation Corps (CCC), accusing the government of creating "forced labor camps" to militarize American youth.

The Party made "Against the Roosevelt War Budget" one of its chief slogans for an anti-war demonstration in 1936. It continued to denounce all military expenditures well into 1937.

A large portion of the *American League Against War and Fascism* was drawn from religious and pacifist circles that were either willing to overlook the Communists' support of some wars, or did not realize that the Party opposed ONLY imperialist wars.

Among many Americans the same kind of attitude exists today as it did when Alexander Bittelman demanded *"Not a cent, not a man, for armaments and war!"*[7]

On October 5, 1937, President Roosevelt warned that America's isolationism would not protect the nation if aggression continued to go unchecked, and he spoke out in behalf of collective security.

America was not prepared for the war that ensued.

Communists have not been idle since World War II. They have infiltrated America's college campuses and have had many opportunities to speak, distribute literature, and propagandize students in Marxism-Leninism.

Today, the United States is the Number One target of the Soviet Spies. From their areas of influence, American Communists have produced Julius Rosenberg, Morton Sobell, the Walker Navy family spy ring, and a whole barrage of others willing and able to betray vital secrets to the Soviet Union. Never in history has a nation been under such a

competent and highly organized attack by highly profes-
sional, well-trained agents who are . . . suave, articulate,
poised, and aggressive. They speak English well and are able
to make direct and personal contact with unsuspecting American businessmen, executives and employees.[8]

They strive to stir mass agitation and build pressure
around specific issues or events, such as the Viet Nam war,
South African apartheid or a racial incident in which "police
brutality" is charged, which will give them the greatest pub-
licity. This tactic has been widely used in America's "peace"
and anti-nuclear demonstrations.[9]

"We are the young and aggressive," Nikita Krushchev
said. "We will wipe the memory of capitalism from the face of
the earth!" Communism fully intends to conquer the world.
"When we conquer the United States," Krushchev is reported to
have said, *"Sixty million Americans must be removed."*

According to the American Tract Society (ATS), an
evangelical pastor in Salem, Oregon, was approached by a
member of the Communist party who boasted that the
Communists have a complete record of pastors and members
of churches in their files ready for action—at the appropriate
time![10]

The ATS quotes an official publication of the Un-
American Activities Committee of the House of Representatives, which points out that if Communism should come to
the United States it would mean that:

1. If you belong to a church, you must prepare for
   persecution.
2. The Communists would destroy every copy of the
   Bible they could find.
3. It would be illegal for your children to attend Sunday
   School.
4. The Communists would indoctrinate your children in
   atheism.
5. Church weddings, funerals, and baptisms would be
   illegal.
6. Missionary work would be absolutely forbidden.[11]

Communism would strip us of our belief in God, our

heritage of freedom, and our trust in justice, mercy, and free enterprise of all citizens. Instead we would become Communist slaves.

In order to resist Communism **individual citizens must**:
1. Be more alert to the dangers of Communism—its true nature and tactics.
2. Learn to identify acts of sabotage, espionage, or subversive conspiracy against our government. Any information should be reported immediately to the FBI.
3. Exercise your right to vote—help elect candidates of integrity. Pray for Christians to run for office.
4. Work to eliminate poverty, discrimination and disease, which enable the Communists to pose as champions of reform.
5. Respect human dignity—Communism and individual rights cannot coexist.
6. Take time to learn more about the basic traditions of America—our history, our national heroes—such as George Washington, Abraham Lincoln, Thomas Paine, Nathan Hale, Patrick Henry, and Benjamin Franklin—and our democratic traditions. Teach your children. A young person knowledgeable of our heritage will not follow the appeals of Communist traitors.
7. Basic to the fight against Communism is faith in a loving God, who leads men to higher levels of personal dignity, morality, and honor. Spiritual faith has always been the strength of America.[12]

A known Communist in San Francisco said that besides *giving one-third of his day to Communism*, he also *gave half of his income*.

Do you give to the cause of Christ and the spread of His gospel as if your life depended on it? You had better, for it does!

This phrase from America's past is a good one for us to remember: *"Pray and keep your powder dry!"*

We must not forget: *"The price of liberty is the ability to defend it!"*

Chapter 10

Communist Goals

QUOTES FROM COMMUNIST LEADERS

". . . The Communist Party cannot be neutral toward religion. It stands for science, and all religion is opposed to science."　　　　　Joseph Stalin, September 7, 1927

"*The policy of Russia is changeless* . . . Its methods, its tactics, its maneuvers may change, but the polar star of its policy—*world domination*—is a fixed star."　　　　Karl Marx, 1867

"Religion . . . is the opium of the people."
　　　　　　　　　　　　　　　　Karl Marx, 1844

". . . there can be no policy of universal freedom in our country, i.e., the freedom of speech, press, etc., for the bourgeoisie."　　　　Joseph Stalin, November 7, 1920

"The theory of the Communists may be summed up in the single sentence: *abolition of private property*."
　　　　　　　Karl Marx, *Communist Manifesto*, 1848

"*Abolition of the family!* Even the most radical flare up at this infamous proposal of the Communists."
　　　　　　　Karl Marx, *Communist Manifesto*, 1848

The bourgeois family will vanish . . . with the vanishing of capital."   Karl Marx

"From 1842 to 1847 Marx 'considered himself to be primarily a crusading journalist.' "
Saul K. Padover, *Karl Marx, On Freedom of the Press*

GOALS OF THE COMMUNIST MANIFESTO, 1848:

1. Abolition of property in land and application of all rents to public purposes.
2. A heavy progressive income tax.
3. Abolition of all right of inheritance.
4. Confiscation of the property of emigrants and rebels.
5. Centralization of credit in the hands of the State.
6. Centralization of the means of communication and transport.
7. Factories and instruments of production, owned by the state.
8. Equal liability of **all** to labor. Establishment of industrial armies, especially for agriculture.
9. Combination of agriculture with manufacturing industries; gradual abolition of the distinction between town and county.
10. Free education for all children in public schools. Abolition of factory labor for children. Education and material production to be combined.
The Communist Manifesto, Sec. 2

"The Communists disdain to conceal their views and aims. They openly declare that their ends can be attained only by the forcible overthrow of all existing social conditions . . . The proletarians have nothing to lose but their chains. They have a world to win."
Karl Marx, *Communist Manifesto*, Sec. 3

"Instead of the conservative motto: 'A fair day's wages for a fair day's work!' they ought to inscribe . . . the revolu-

tionary watchword: 'Abolition of the wages system.' "
Karl Marx, June 27, 1865

". . . **Socialism is bound sooner or later to ripen into Communism**, whose banner bears the motto: "From each according to his ability, to each according to his needs."
Lenin, 1917

"**Give me four years to teach the children and the seed I have sown will never be uprooted.**"
Lenin, quoted by *N.Y. Times Magazine*

"The bourgeois clap-trap about the family and education, about the hallowed co-relation of parent and child . . . disgusting . . . all family ties among the proletariat are torn asunder, and their children transformed into simple articles of commerce and instruments of labor."
Karl Marx, *Communist Manifesto*, Sec 3

"Do not deny the **terror**. Don't minimize the **evils** of a Revolution."
Lenin quoted in *Lincoln Steffens, a Biography* (1975)

Communism repudiates eternal truths, repudiates religion and morality instead of refashioning them, and is thus at odds with the whole course of historical evolution."
Karl Marx, *"The Communist Manifesto"* p. 51.

"Every man who occupies himself with the construction of a God, or merely even agrees to it, prostitutes himself in the worst way . . ." Lenin, *Socialism and Religion,* 1905, Vol. II.

"Religion is the opium of the people. Religion is a kind of spiritual vodka . . ."
Lenin, *Socialism and Religion,* 1905, Vol. II.

". . . woman continues to be a domestic slave, because petty housework crushes, strangles, stultifies and degrades her, chains her to the kitchen and to the nursery, and wastes her labor on barbarously unproductive, petty, nerve-wracking, stultifying and crushing drudgery. **The real emancipation of women, real Communism** will begin only when a mass struggle . . . is started against this petty domestic economy, or rather when it is transformed . . . into Socialist economy."[1]   Lenin.

In his introduction to a later edition of the *Manifesto*, Engles explains in which sense he and Marx made use of the word *Socialism* in that historic document: *Socialism, in contradistinction to Communism, was for them a movement among the workers* or among the bourgeoise whose *aim was to do away with poverty.* For the authors of the Manifesto, *Socialism was the doctrine of those who championed different kinds of Utopian systems which appealed*—just as the former schemes appealed—*to the "educated" classes,* i.e., to the bourgeoisie.   *The Communist Manifesto.* p. 210.

COMMUNIST OBJECTIVE—ERADICATING RELIGION FROM SOCIETY

"Every religious idea, every idea of a god, even flirting with the idea of a god, is unutterable vileness of the most dangerous kind . . . millions of sins, filthy deeds, acts of violence . . . are far less dangerous than the subtle spiritual idea of a god."   Lenin

"The religion of the workers has no God, because it seeks to restore the divinity of Man."   Karl Marx

History has shown us that Communist regimes inevitably seek to either eradicate the Church or to subvert it . . . the Church's existence is repugnant to them. Allegiance to God prevents total allegiance to the State which, according to Marx, is the vehicle for *transformation of man into God*.

The Communists **cannot** tolerate this limitation on their absolute power. Thus, in the Soviet Union all but a tiny percentage of churches have been closed and religious affiliation routinely brings the loss of precious privileges and sometimes brings more serious persecution.

Sixty-five years of applied Marxist-Leninist doctrine have shown that Communism will not accept co-existence with any religion that does not concede supreme authority to it. To the extent that Marxist-Leninst regimes allow churches to operate they do so because they are forced to, as in Poland, or for tactical reasons aimed at the ultimate objective of eradicating religion from society.

There were 77,000 churches in 1914, before the revolution during which thousands of Christians were martyred. Today there are 7,000 churches in all of the USSR. All are under the control of the government. So much for religious freedom.[2]

The United Nations, New York

Chapter 11

The United Nations—
Haven For Spies

"The extent to which the Soviet KGB has infiltrated the UN was the subject of *The Intelligence Report*, dated 21 March 1984. The increasingly-bold use of the United Nations by the Soviet Union to promote its own interest in the world and as a base for espionage within the United States is causing increasing concern in Washington.

"The FBI wants to increase its counter-intelligence force by approximately 25% in the next two years to fight the growing Soviet-bloc spy threat.

"The force has already been increased by 30% during the past three years. **The biggest target for foreign spies is the American high-technology industries** that have key defense and industrial applications—particularly companies dealing with computers, aerospace, and fibre-optic communications. 'Star Wars' technology would obviously be one of the areas of interest to them.

"In the United Nations' headquarters, approximately 3,000 citizens of communist countries work in their national missions or in the UN Secretariat. According to Arkady Shevchenko, former Soviet Under Secretary General at the Secretariat until his defection in 1978, **more than a third of this total are KGB agents!**"[1]

"Shevchenko and another Soviet defector, Igor Glagolev, report that the position of Special Assistant to the UN

Secretary General is 'traditionally' held by a medium-rank KBG officer. *'This assistant,'* adds Glagolev, *'practically controls the whole staff of the UN.'*

"The FBI believes that the Soviet agents with diplomatic status at the UN are *primarily interested in recruiting spies.* Through Soviet officials in the UN personnel departments, the KGB is able to get personal information on UN diplomats who might be co-opted.

"According to Shevchenko, the Soviets operate highly-sophisticated electronic spying equipment from a mansion owned by their UN Mission in Glen Cove, New York. The purpose is to monitor long-distance phone conversations and spy on industry in the area.

Our diplomats in Communist countries are highly restricted in their travel. They can only go to certain areas and must often be accompanied by a Soviet staff person, likely a KGB agent. Meanwhile, here in the USA the Soviet diplomats can freely travel anywhere, with no restrictions. The *Intelligence Digest* pointed out:

UN Secretariat employees can freely travel anywhere in the US, in cars bearing US license plates, making it almost impossible to monitor all of their activities. Mr. Shevchenko explains that Soviet KGB agents in the Secretariat take advantage of this privilege to conduct high-technology espionage operations on a wide scale.

"The FBI is also aware of extensive contacts with 'illegals'—Soviet or communist-bloc-nationals who are in the US with false documents or under false pretenses!"

"If the US is not prepared to leave the UN—or expel it from New York—there are, nevertheless, increasing calls for a cut in funding and for measures which would reduce Soviet influence in the body, limit its potential as a base for espionage, and prevent it from fomenting terrorist wars. American patience with the UN may, finally, be running out."[2]

It is time our government decided to force the Soviets to adhere to the same rules for diplomatic activities. Our people must be given unlimited travel in the Soviet-block or we should restrict the travel of all Soviet citizens, and citizens from Communist countries within the United States.

It is time for equal treatment. In recent years, the U.S. built a new embassy in Moscow, and the Soviets built a new embassy in Washington, D.C. In Moscow, we were allowed to build on the very lowest spot in the city, while the United States gave the Soviets the highest piece of ground in Washington, D.C., which makes it ideal for electronic spying.

Both embassies were started at the same time, but Soviets delayed our construction—we should have put a halt to theirs, but we made it very easy—theirs was finished years ahead of ours.

It is time for our government to limit activities of UN personnel. At the present time they conduct espionage on a wide scale, recruit spies, conduct press conferences, help instigate events such as the "nuclear freeze" movement and the "South African apartheid" movement—affecting Americans who are naively taken in by Communist manipulators— and influencing and sometimes, it seems, even directing American policy.

THE USA's STAKE IN THE UN

At the heart of US concern is that the United States pays about 25 percent of the total UN budget—far more than any other country. Through 1985, the US spent almost $15 billion on the United Nations through assessments and voluntary contributions. Six countries as shown in the UN Assessment chart, paid 67.8 percent, **the remaining 153 countries paid 32.2 percent.**

US officials say that *UN bureaucrats often do little real work* between the hectic annual sessions and are *paid 25 percent more than the average US civil servant*, when expenses, living allowances and tax breaks are included.

What do we gain from all this expenditure?

Vernon Walters, US Ambassador to the United Nations, noted: **"the so-called 'non-aligned' countries in the General Assembly last year (in 1984) voted 86.2 percent** *against* **the US on key issues."**[3]

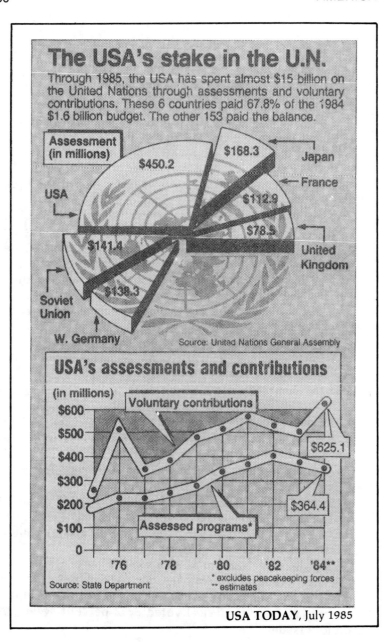

The USA's stake in the U.N.

Through 1985, the USA has spent almost $15 billion on the United Nations through assessments and voluntary contributions. These 6 countries paid 67.8% of the 1984 $1.6 billion budget. The other 153 paid the balance.

Assessment (in millions)

$450.2 — USA
$168.3 — Japan
$112.9 — France
$78.5 — United Kingdom
$141.4 — Soviet Union
$138.3 — W. Germany

Source: United Nations General Assembly

USA's assessments and contributions

(in millions)

Voluntary contributions — $625.1

Assessed programs* — $364.4

'76   '78   '80   '82   '84**

Source: State Department

* excludes peacekeeping forces
** estimates

USA TODAY, July 1985

Upset over left-leaning politics and fiscal irresponsibility, the US officially withdrew from UNESCO, the United Nations Educational, Scientific and Cultural Organization.

The ruckus over the US withdrawal from UNESCO in 1984 symbolizes US feelings about the use of the body not only as a forum for anti-Americanism but also as a haven for Communist spies.

"The UN is dominated by a loose coalition—with strong Soviet support—that is fundamentally hostile to the US," adds Charles Lichenstein, a former deputy US Ambassador to the UN from 1981-84, presently working for the Heritage Foundation, "and that situation is not going to change any time soon."

"The UN on too many issues has subverted the national interest for a Marxist majority in the UN," says Howard Phillips, head of the Conservative Caucus.

Phillips concluded: "**Not only is it a haven for spies, it's a source of assistance for terrorists all over the world.**"[4]

Young children are quickly indoctrinated into Communist ideology, including a hatred of the "imperialist" United States.

Chapter 12

Threat To Our Hemisphere

Secretary of Defense, Caspar Weinberger, reminded Americans in his 1985 report on Soviet Military Power: "It is incumbent upon the United States and its Allies to have a full and precise understanding of the Soviet challenge, as we take the steps necessary to preserve our freedom . . . ."

"Ours is a free society; the Soviet Union is not. The updated facts presented," Secretary Weinberger said, in his 1983 report: "leave no doubt as to the USSR's dedication to achieving military superiority in all fields."

"It is our duty to have a full awareness of Soviet military growth, modernization and capabilities . . . and to shape our defense forces and our deterrent capabilities accordingly. We can do no less if we are to provide fully and wisely for our security, and that of our Allies."

"Ours is a formidable task, made more difficult by a decade of our neglect coupled with two decades of massive Soviet increases. But, we and our Allies can accomplish the task if . . .

1. We have the will,
2. The courage, and
3. The resolution possessed in ample measure by our predecessors who won our freedom, and who kept it for us all."

"This is at once our most precious heritage and our most solemn responsibility to posterity."

The Secretary's report stated: "The USSR's combat

operations have continued to expand in Afghanistan, and now involve more than 105,000 Soviet troops with some of the newest Soviet weapons."

"From Indochina to the Caribbean, the USSR has continued to expand its global military presence. To cite just one example, a Soviet Navy task force operated in the Caribbean and Gulf of Mexico from November 1982 to (the present)."[1]

CUBAN THREAT TO OUR HEMISPHERE

1959—PANAMA
80-100 fully armed guerrillas leave Cuba to invade Panama. OAS investigating committee, using aircraft and patrol boats, force invading forces to surrender.

1961—PERU
Peru alleges Cuban intervention and subversion. OAS Council confirms Cuban subversion.

1961—COLOMBIA
Alleges Cuba a threat to peace and security of hemisphere. **Castro government excluded from participation in OAS.**

1962—CUBA
Cuba allows installation of nuclear weapons by USSR. OAS authorizes individual and collective measures including force to resist Cuban Marxism.

1963—1964 VENEZUELA
Alleges Cuba depositing arms in Venezuela. OAS verifies facts as true, votes sanctions against Cuba. In 1964, a meeting of the OAS Ministers of Foreign Affairs established that: "the Republic of Venezuela has been the target of a series of actions sponsored and directed by the government of Cuba, **openly intended to . . overthrow, sabotage, assault.**"

1967—VENEZUELA AND BOLIVIA

Allegations of Cuba intervention. OAS condemns Cuba, extends sanctions including cutoff of government sales and credits to Cuba.[2]

COMMUNISM IN CENTRAL AMERICA

The important conclusions of the *Bipartisan Commission's Report* submitted to President Reagan on January 11, 1984 were:

• "It is in the national security interest of the US to prevent a Communist Central America—the ability of the United States to sustain a tolerable balance of power on the global scene at a manageable cost depends on the inherent security of its land borders . . .

"Therefore, the advance of Soviet and Cuban power and a further projection of Soviet and Cuban power in the region require us to defend against security threats near our borders, we would face a difficult choice between unpalatable alternatives . . .

"Either . . .

1. A permanently increased defense burden,
2. Or see our capacity to defend distant troubled spots reduced,
3. And as a result have to reduce important commitments elsewhere in the world." (meaning Europe, the Middle East and East Asia, Chap. 6)[3]

• "Nicaragua violated its commitments to implement democracy. Its export of subversion offers a forecast of what other Marxist/Leninist regimes would do. Additional Marxist/Leninist regimes in Central America could be expected to:

1. Expand their armed forces,
2. Bring in large numbers of Cuban and other Soviet bloc advisers,
3. Develop sophisticated agencies of internal repression and external subversion, and

4. Sharpen polarizations, both within individual countries and regionally."[4]

• **"Consequences of this process would be severe** in human as well as geopolitical terms: this would almost surely produce refugees, perhaps millions of them, many of whom would seek entry into the United States . . .

• **"The crisis is serious**, and the US response must include support for democratic development, improved living conditions, diplomacy, and security assistance."

• **"The level of effort must be increased substantially**."

"The United States cannot isolate itself from the regional turmoil. The crisis is on our doorstep."[5]

EL SALVADOR: A DEMOCRATIC REVOLUTION

In the mid-1970's an indigenous guerrilla force began receiving extensive support from Nicaragua. The unification of the Salvadoran guerrillas was coordinated by Fidel Castro. Promising them increased support if they would forget past rivalries and forge a united front, Castro brought Salvadoran guerrilla leaders to Havana. This led to the creation of the Farabundo Marti National Liberation Front (FMLN), in which five previously separate guerrilla military factions banded together.

The Salvadoran guerrillas are open about their Marxist-Leninist leanings, as shown in this poster marking the tenth anniversary, 1970-1980.[6]

The Salvadoran guerrillas receive the bulk of their arms, ammunition, and supplies from Nicaragua. The Soviet Union also contributes to the guerrilla causes through its extensive *"Active Measures"* program.

"Active Measures" is a term used by the Soviet KGB for its program of overt and covert deception operations, including use of forged documents, front groups, agents of influence,

State Department photo

The poster proclaims, "Revolution or death! The armed people will triumph!"

and clandestine broadcasting.

The guerrilla's goal in applying Soviet disinformation, propaganda, and deception techniques is to gain sympathy for their cause. At the same time they wish to sway international and United States public opinion against the Salvadoran government and U.S. economic and military assistance.

In February 1982, Hector Oqueli told the *New York Times*: "We have to win the war in the United States."[7]

Moscow's Radio *Peace and Progress,* a well known disinformation outlet, has broadcast such inflammatory allegations as:

- "The CIA kidnaps children of Salvadoran refugees in Honduras . . . some are sent to special schools for brainwashing. Others . . . are sent to CIA research centers. Here they are used as guinea pigs."[8]
- "US military advisers participate in torturing Salvadoran rebels and prisoners . . ."[9]
- "Everything that is known . . . indicates the Yankee CIA, corporation of murderers, is implicated in the death of Torrijos."[10]

Salvadoran citizens line up to vote during presidential elections on 25 March 1984.

In October 1979, reform-minded Salvadoran military officers overthrew the authoritarian government of General Carlos Romero. Romero was replaced by a civilian-military junta that pledged social and economic reforms and democratic elections. The successive governments of El Salvador have worked to follow through on these pledges.[11]

An April, 1983, guerrilla radio broadcast declared: "Our

forces will start sabotage against the dictatorship's war economy during the next days." This sabotage has included the destruction of bridges and electrical towers, as well as the cash crops so vital to the Salvadoran economy. The government's budget has been severely strained to repair damage caused by this systematic sabotage.[12]

Since 1982, the people of El Salvador have shown their support for the democratic process by going to the polls *three times* in the face of threats and harassment by the guerrillas.

Hundreds of international observers attested to the *legitimacy* of the elections. Jose Napoleon Duarte, a reform minded Christian Democrat, previously jailed and sent into exile by the military, was elected President on 25 March 1984.

Commenting on the legitimacy of the electorial process, the official publication of the Archdiocese of San Salvador said: ". . . one can say with absolute certainty that three elections in a two-year period [have occurred] . . . in which the people have expressed their will, their faith in democracy, their desire for peace, their rejection of violence, and their intrinsic condemnation of the guerrillas."[13]

GUATEMALA—A TARGET OF CASTRO'S SUBVERSION

In Guatemala, Castro has provided training and some financial support to three guerrilla factions, although he has not succeeded in unifying them to the extent he did in El Salvador.

Guerrilla weapons, posters, and flags were captured by the Guatemalan armed forces. The guerrillas make no attempt to disguise their ties to international communism.[14]

COLOMBIAN DRUG SMUGGLERS—A NEW THREAT

A disturbing aspect of the current Castro offensive is the apparent use of money generated by narcotics to supply arms for guerrillas. The drugs move northward from Colombia to the United States, at times via Cuba and on at least one occasion via Nicaragua.[15]

State Department photo

The loading of cocaine on a US-bound plane at the Los Brasiles airport in Nicaragua. Photo released during US Congressional hearings in 1984.

In 1981, the Colombian government discovered that the Cubans had been using a narcotics ring to smuggle both arms and funds to Colombian M-19 guerrillas. When the Colombian armed forces and National Police entered the town of Calamar in February 1984, they discovered that the

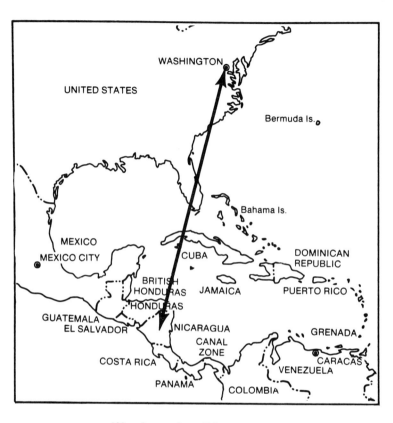

War is raging 5 hours away.

guerrilla Revolutionary Armed Forces of Colombia had campesinos cultivating hundreds of hectares of coca plants.

Recent United States Congressional hearings have established the linkage of Cuba, narcotics, and guerrillas.[46]

US arrest warrants have been issued for one Nicaraguan and several Cuban officials involved in drug trafficking from Colombia.

Reacting to an all-out anti-drug campaign by the Colombian government, the Colombian **drug criminals** have:

- Murdered Colombian government officials

- Bombed the US Embassy
- Issued death threats against:
    - US diplomats and their families,
    - Colombian President Betancur and his cabinet, and
    - Members of the Colombian Supreme Court.

The emerging alliance between drug smugglers and arms dealers in support of terrorists and guerrillas is a troublesome new threat to the Western hemisphere.

Chapter 13

Communism In Romania

Romania, once a primary agricultural supplier for Central Europe now suffers from a bankrupt economy. Not only are basic foodstuffs such as sugar, eggs, cooking oil, flour, and meat rationed (when they are available), but so is electricity! *Last winter only one room per household was allowed to be lit—and then with just a 40-watt bulb.* All household appliances including refrigerators, had to be unplugged.

Upon crossing into Romania, the poverty is one of the first things a person notices: there are very few cars and many horse or ox-drawn carts. *Gasoline is rationed at eight gallons a month per car—even this is often not available.* According to one Eastern European Bible Mission (EEBM) contact, *this is the government's way of controlling the people by immobilizing them.*[1]

This control is felt in many other ways. Private printing presses and photocopy machines are illegal. Even *all typewriters are registered*, thus inhibiting the production of "unauthorized" materials such as Christian literature.

A report from Eastern European Bible Mission November/December, 1985, newsletter begins with a remark by a Romanian Christian to an EEBM missionary. "Living in Romania is like living on a volcano—you never know when it will erupt."

The report tells of life under Communist control.

Church buildings have been leveled by authorities. The Christian Response International (CRI) July/August, 1985 newsletter reported: Another Baptist church comes down! *Two days after President Reagan requested renewal of Romania's favored-nation trade status, Romanian authorities tore down the church.*

May 1985
CRI photo

Demolished Giulesti Baptist Church

CRI's report continued: "On June 3, 1983, remodeling of the Giulesti Baptist Church in Bucharest, Romania, ended when the facility was totally demolished by order of the police. In an effort to prevent the destruction of their building, more than seventy members of the Baptist congregation had occupied the building around the clock for four days. On Monday afternoon, police came to the building and physically carried out men, women and young people. Reports indicate two elders and the pastor Rev. Buni Cocar were arrested. Cocar was given 24 hours to pack and leave Bucharest. According to reliable sources the two elders were severely beaten by the Romanian police.'

The church had been bulldozed to the ground because government officials said the small addition made to the building measured four inches beyond the approved permit. No one from the church had been allowed to check the accuracy of measurements.

Constant threats against church leaders, and the loss of education and work opportunities for Christians, has resulted in growth of the number and strength of believers in Romania.

The Eastern European Bible Mission (EEBM) newsletter reports: "The largest denomination is the Romanian Orthodox Church. But most of the spiritual vitality is in evangelical groups such as the Baptists, Pentecostals, and the Lord's Army—a secret lay movement of 200,000 to 500,000 believers within the Orthodox Church."

"The growth of these groups does not excite the atheistic rulers, who do everything possible to make life hard for Christians. One way has been via a severe crackdown at the borders in the last 18 months . . . as a result, some Western missions have stopped their literature delivery to Romania. This, in turn, has resulted in an even more critical shortage of Bibles within the country . . . "

THE GOSPEL ON TOILET PAPER

According to EEBM, "The Romanian authorities were *not* intentionally trying to put a portion of Scripture in every home."

"It seems that a legal shipment of 20,000 Bibles to the Hungarian Reformed Church in Romania has turned up—processed into toilet paper by the Romanian government!

"Several years ago, under Western pressure, the Romanian President, Nicolae Ceausescu, and his regime gave permission for the *legal importation of 20,000 Bibles* for Hungarian-speaking citizens in Romania.

"However the fate of the Bibles was shrouded in mystery for some time. Romanian Church officials, *who are government appointed*, could never give a proper accounting of the Bibles' distribution. Congregations never heard about their existence.

"And now finally, after a long silence, the Bibles have reappeared—in the form of toilet paper!

"The 20,000 Hungarian Bibles sent by the World Reformed Alliance, were redirected by Romanian authorities to a paper mill for recycling. The mill was **not** able to do a very thorough job—*because of the excellent quality of the western bibliophile paper*. Shreds of paper, with original words and letters, remained almost intact in the final toilet paper products."

The EEBM report continues: "Reliable reports state that Romanian President Ceausescu has also ordered the confiscation of all Hungarian Bibles from the homes of the 120,000 Hungarians in the Moldavia district."

Dr. Alexander Havadtoy, of Yale Divinity School, displays Romanian toilet paper made from Bibles.

EEBM photo

According to CRI's July/August, 1985 newsletter, *Response*, "Former U.S. Ambassador to Romania David Funderburk, Rep. Mark Siljander (R/MI), Rep. Chris Smith (R/NJ), Senator Paul Simon (D/MI), Rep. Bob Dornan (R/CA), Rep. Dan Burton (R/IN) and Dr. Alexander Havadtoy joined CRI Executive Director Jeff Collins in a Capitol Hill news conference on religious repression in Romania.

"The Congressmen joined CRI in protesting Romania's continued demolition of Christian churches, the arrest of the Romanian Baptist layleader Constantine Sfatcu, the con-

tinued imprisonment of the Seventh-day Adventist believer
Dorei Catarama and the astounding revelation that the
Romanian government had recycled a *legal* shipment of
20,000 Bibles into toilet paper.

"Ambassador Funderburk, who announced his resigna-
tion on May 13, 1985, because of what he felt was "Romania's abysmal record on human rights," praised CRI's intervention on behalf of Romanian Christians."

More than fifty journalists covered the news conference, including such major media as *Time* magazine and
Associated Press . . . but did **you** hear about it? CBN (Christian Broadcasting Network) interviews of CRI staff have
appeared on The 700 Club.

Nestled between the Soviet Union and Bulgaria, Romania's 21.5 million people live under one of the most repres-
sive regimes in Eastern Europe. The Soviet Union has basi-
cally allowed Romanian President Ceausescu to retain his
nation's image as having loosened its ties with Moscow over
the last 30 years, while keeping him under political control
of the USSR. Who is being deceived by this charade of independence? Americans?

In sharp contrast to supposed freedoms from Soviet bloc
ties stand the reality of an official propaganda sign which
proclaims the anniversary of the Revolution and liberation
from Western imperialists.[2]

Oppression of individuals, coupled with persecution of
church leaders and believers, makes us question **why** . . .

Why would the President and our legislators grant *most-
favored-nation* status, and its resulting economic benefits to
Romania? Why not give these benefits to Canada or a supportive NATO ally? **Why** to a Communist controlled
country?

Perhaps it's happened because many Americans don't
know it's happening, nor what is involved.

It's time for Americans to speak up and demand an end
to our tax dollars supporting Communism and Communist
nations!

This photograph indicates the Communist message,
denouncing imperialists, is far from secretive.

Chapter 14

Twenty Wars!

At this moment, there are some 20 wars and insurgencies being waged at different locations around the globe. These real and potential areas of violence endanger our national interests . . .[1]

FLASH POINTS

"Flash points" are those parts of the world where a confrontation between the superpowers is considered a possibility, even though the regional conflict may begin *without* direct superpower involvement.

A Department of Defense (DOD) paper points out that the African continent is in considerable turmoil—including Angola and Ethiopia which have between them 40,000 Cuban combat troops and advisors, and several thousand Soviet advisors. Libya's Colonel Qadaffi's radical policies must not be overlooked.

In Europe, we have two potential flash points: Berlin, a city we would be unwise to forget, and Poland. The brutal murder of Father Jerzy Popieuluszko by four Polish secret policemen demonstrates the true nature of the Polish government.

Today, some call for limiting our presence on that continent and for cutting back on our contributions to NATO. Our value there is shown in the fact that Western Europe has been at peace for a longer period than at any time since the Roman Empire.

The Middle East continues to be troublesome. The war between Iran and Iraq is one of the most serious conflicts in the world today, which could destabilize that area of the world. Because of the terrorism we Americans endured while helping the Lebanese government in Beirut, we are particularly aware of the conflict there.

In Afghanistan, the Soviets, with over 115,000 troops, have been surprised and embarrassed by the men and women freedom fighters who have defended their country against the Soviet invaders for over five years.

The Soviet army is deployed in large numbers along the Sino-Soviet border and in growing numbers on Sakhalin Island and the four occupied islands of the Kurile chain.

North Korea occupies a unique position within the Communist bloc. It is one of the most closed, closely controlled societies in the world. Each year it commits 24 percent of its income to the development of its military power. Males are drafted for five to ten years.

In recent years we have discovered three tunnels dug by the North Koreans underneath the Demilitarized Zone— one of which was more than 50 meters below the surface of the ground—dug through solid granite. These tunnels were of such a substantial size they could have been used to infiltrate large numbers of troops into the South in a short period of time, and there is reason to believe there may be more.

THE CHALLENGE

The Soviets have 194 Army Divisions compared to our 24. They have a manpower pool of over **nine million** that has completed military training within the last five years.

We have four Army Divisions in Europe now, compared with some 30 Soviet divisions. In virtually every area of conventional and nuclear power, the Soviet Union outnumbers the United States. When President Reagan asks Congress to approve a defense budget, he is basing it on a recognized threat.

Kremlin leaders hope that ultimately the United States could become so preoccupied with turmoil in the Central American and Caribbean region that it would be less able militarily and politically to oppose Soviet goals in other key areas of the world.

The consequences of a Soviet-aligned Central America would be severe and immediate. The United States would be faced with complicated defense planning due to Communist expansion into Mexico and the need to keep sea lanes open in Panama.[2]

The United States is responding to this challenge by providing economic and military assistance programs . . . so that the countries have the capability to defend themselves.

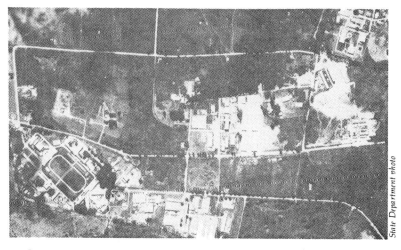

State Department photo

Soviet intelligence collection facility near Havana, Cuba. This listening post enables the Soviets to monitor US communications.

Voice of Americanism Photo

Marxist revolutionaries in Central America are desperately generating support for Nicaragua's Moscow-supported terrorism.

Chapter 15

Communism In Nicaragua

A White House paper on the *Freedom Fighters in Nicaragua*, issued in February 1985, stated:

• "Sandinista armed subversion began in August 1979, and freedom fighter operations in Nicaragua began in the spring of 1982. This demonstrates that the freedom fighters are a defensive response to counter the Nicaraguan aggression and, therefore, legitimate under the UN and OAS Charters.

• "Majorities in both houses of the US Congress agree with the Democratic-led House Intelligence Committee report of May 1983, which summarized the facts of Nicaraguan armed subversion against its neighbors.

• "Concerning US support for the freedom fighters in Nicaragua, the Administration does not comment officially. However, you can draw your own conclusions from the sentence in the State of the Union address. 'It is essential that the Congress continue all facets of our assistance in Central America.

• "If there were no freedom fighters in Nicaragua, it would be logical to expect the Sandinista regime to . . . surreptitiously infiltrate 5,000 . . . to 15,000 of its 119,000-strong trained military forces into El Salvador, Guatemala, and other target countries. This could mean dramatically increased danger and loss of life and could undo the progress made.

• "The President will remind the Congress of what he told the nation on national television in May 1984:

• "*If we . . . provide too little help, our choice will be a Communist Central America* with additional Communist military bases on the mainland of this hemisphere and Communist subversion spreading southward and northward."

"*This Communist subversion poses the threat that 100 million people, from Panama to the open border on our south, could come under the control of Pro-Soviet regimes.*"[1]

Oliver North, Deputy Director, for Political-Military Affairs, of the National Security Council, conducted a White House Briefing in February 1986, on the dangerous situation in the Western Hemisphere. War is raging just five hours from Washington, DC. We dare not ignore the threat to our security!

Mr. North revealed that Soviet ships were operating just 14 miles off the Louisiana coast in 1985! A Soviet long-range (Bear) reconnaissance aircraft flying near the Virginia coast was intercepted by Air Force fighter planes in 1985. His briefing revealed Soviet-made ships at Lourdes, Cuba, 97 miles from the U.S. border. Here they regularly intercept and monitor our phone calls. We cannot take these reports lightly!

We must be concerned about the media misrepresentation of Marxist/Leninist guerillas as "freedom fighters" or "reformers", or other terms which do not reveal their true identity as Communists.

We must question why the media is pro-communist. Information is available to the media, yet they *choose* not to tell the truth about the Communist buildup and threat.

STATE DEPARTMENT REPORT REVEALS SANDINISTA AND PLO TERRORIST CONNECTION

An unclassified State Department report, *The Sandinistas and Middle Easstern Radicals*, dated August, 1985, reveals Sandinista participation in Middle East aircraft hijacking and terrorism in 1970, and continuing relations with these groups in the 1980's.

This report notes . . . the relationship between the Sandinistas and radical Middle Eastern groups . . . including terrorist elements. Their ties with the Palestine Liberation Organization reach back more than ten years before the revolution in Nicaragua. Libya has given the Sandinista both pre- and post-revolution aid, at first in conjunction with or through the Palestine Liberation Organization (PLO), and eventually through its own agreements with the Sandinista government. More recently, the Sandinistas have developed closer ties with Iran.

The report describes the Tri-Continental Conference held in 1966, in Havana, Cuba, when Fidel Castro brought together 500 delegates from radical leftist groups around the world, for what they called the global revolutionary movement.[2]

In the months following the Tri-Continental Conference guerrilla training camps appeared in Cuba, the Soviet Union, Lebanon, and Libya. Members of the PLO were among the first to be trained in the Cuban and Soviet camps, which generally lasted six months.

The camps provided practical training in the use of weapons and explosives, and techniques of warfare including:
- blowing up bridges, vehicles, munitions dumps,
- planting personnel mines,
- the rudiments of chemical warfare,
- marksmanship and camouflage,
- the use and maintenance of Soviet equipment, such as rockets and shoulderborne missile launchers.

The ideological indoctrination focused on the theories of Marx and Lenin. Lecture topics included: "Russian Ties to the Third World", "The Struggle Against Imperialism" and "Soviet Contribution to Palestinian Liberation."[3]

Upon graduation, PLO guerrillas set up camps of their own for training terrorists, at first in Lebanon and later in Libya. Reportedly among the Nicaraguans trained in the Lebanon camps in 1969 was Tomas Borge, Interior Minister. Also in 1969, Sandinista representative, Benito Escobar, arranged with three PLO representatives in Mexico City, for joint PLO-Cuban training in Lebanon for a contingent of 50-70 Sandinistas.[4]

The State Department report contains photographs of three aircraft hijacked by the PLO in September 1970. According to a Sandinista spokesman, Sandinistas participated in the triple hijacking. Some 40 passengers were held hostage, but were eventually released, after the destruction of the aircraft.[5]

State Department photo

PLO who hijacked three aircraft in September 1970. Sandinistas participated in the triple hijacking. 40 passengers were held hostage, but released after the destruction of the aircraft.

The PLO and the Sandinistas issued a joint communique on February 5, 1978, affirming the "bonds of solidarity which exist between the two revolutionary organizations."[6]

This communique was followed by a Democratic Front for the Liberation of Palestine (DFLP)-Sandinista National Liberation Front (FSLN) joint declaration from Havana on

March 6, 1978, which expressed: "**A mutual declaration of war against Yankee Imperialism, and the racist regime of Israel, and the Nicaraguan government.**"[7]

Shortly after the Sandinistas seized power, the PLO was permitted to open an "embassy" in Managua, with the ranking representative holding the title of Ambassador.[8]

In July 1980, Yasser Arafat made a four-day "state visit" to Nicaragua to formalize full diplomatic ties between the Nicaraguan government and the PLO. At a reception in Arafat's honor, Interior Minister Borge said "We say to our brother Arafat that Nicaragua is his land and the PLO cause is the cause of the Sandinistas."

Arafat replied: "The links between us are not new. Your comrades did not come to our country just to train, but also to fight. Your enemies are our enemies."[9]

In a speech at the Cesar Augusto Silva Convention Center (also July 22), standing with Borge and others of the nine Comandantes, Arafat said, "Anyone who threatens Nicaragua will have to face Palestinian combatants."[10]

In November 1980, the PLO provided the Sandinistas with a $12 million loan. In January 1981, a group of PLO pilots were sent to Nicaragua to assist the Sandinistas in flying helicopters and transport aircraft. By May 1981, the PLO was deeply involved in military and guerrilla training activities . . . reports in mid-1982 indicated that PLO officers were involved in special guerilla training in Nicaragua.[11]

By the time the Sandinistas came to power in 1979, they had developed close relationships with Muammar Qadhafi's regime. Tomas Borge and Construction Minister Moises Hassan were key figures in working with Libya. Both were instrumental in obtaining a $100 million loan in 1981. On June 20, 1981, the Sandinistas had a lavish celebration in Managua marking the 11th anniversary of Qadhafi's ouster of U.S. air bases from Libyan territory.[12]

The Libyans have sent arms shipments to the Sandinistas. One arms shipment of 84 tons was intercepted in Brazil during April 1983. Four Libyan planes contained: two dismantled fighter planes, wire-guided missiles, rifles, machine guns, mortars, bazookas, 90mm cannons, eight multiple rocket launchers, five tons of bombs, eight anti-aircraft guns, 600 light artillery rockets, and other crates of military equipment.[13]

The Sandinistas' initial reaction to the discovery of this arms shipment was almost as noteworthy as the shipment itself. The Nicaraguan ambassador to Brazil, Ernesto Gutierrez, stated: "It was a donation from our Libyan comrades, but I do not know what it was."[14]

State Department photo

Soviet-made Libyan transport at Manaus, Brazil, April 1983. Large arms shipments falsely described as "medical supplies for Colombia" were on board. The intended destination was Nicaragua.

BRAZIL ELECTIONS

The *Washington Post*, on November 16, 1985, reported that the Brazilian Democratic Movement Party, the main force in the eight-month-old civilian government, was headed for broad victory in races for control of many of Brazil's key cities. The Party suffered a loss in Sao Paulo, Brazil's largest city with 10 million residents. The winner there was Jania Quadros, who was backed by a conservative coalition. In Rio de Janeiro, Roberto Saturnino Braga of the **Socialist**-oriented Democratic Labor Party won, as generally expected. The Democratic Movement won or was leading in 16 of Brazil's 23 state capitals.

IRAN CONNECTION

Nicaragua's relationship with Iran goes back several years, including the May 1983 visit of Ernesto Cardenal to Iran. Cardenal, the Sandinista Minister of Culture, was given a private audience with the Ayatollah Khomeini, a rarity for westerners. In March 1984, junta member Sergio Ramirez went to Iran to discuss trade and other matters. This visit resulted in a $23 million trade agreement between Nicaragua and Iran.[15]

Mohammed Mirmehdi, Iran's Deputy Foreign Minister, met with Sandinista Comandante and President Daniel Ortega on January 14, 1985.[16]

On January 23, 1985, Prime Minister Mirhussein Musavi went to Nicaragua and met with Daniel Ortega (their third meeting). An ABC news report stated that Prime Minister Musavi is believed to control Iran's terrorist operations.[17]

The Sandinistas admit that an oil deal with Iran was discussed, but they deny that arms shipments were agreed upon. Nevertheless, there were reports on January 25, 1985, that two shiploads of arms were underway from Iran, to be transferred to Nicaraguan ships at some point . . .[18]

HAVEN FOR SUBVERSIVES

The FSLN government has issued Nicaraguan passports to radicals and terrorists of other nationalities, including radicals from the Middle East, Latin America, and Europe, thus enabling them to travel in western countries without their true identities being known.[19]

PLO agents working in Central America and Panama use Nicaragua as their base of operations. The Sandinistas' willingness to provide new documentation and a base from which to travel is undoubtedly one reason why Nicaragua has become a haven for terrorists and radicals from Europe as well as Latin America.[20]

Beyond Sandinista political, military, and economic cooperation with Middle East radical states and the PLO is Nicaragua's connection with international terrorist groups, such as the German Baader-Meinhof Gang, the Italian Red Brigades, and the Basque Homeland and Liberty organization (ETA).

The middle eastern entities Nicaragua has chosen to deal with—the PLO, Libya, and Iran—have had known involvement in terrorist activity, including the planning, training, financing, and implementation of terrorist acts. Sandinista ties with this network pose increasing danger of violence for the Western Hemisphere.

State Department photo

US Navy F-4 intercepts Soviet BEAR-D reconnaissance aircraft 42 miles off the Virginia coast.

Chapter 16

Growing Soviet Investment

Nicaraguan President Daniel Ortega's first trip to Moscow took place in April 1980, *only nine months after the Sanidinistas came to power . . . and at a time when the United States was providing Nicaragua with extensive economic aid.* One month earlier, a number of agreements were reached between the USSR and Nicaragua, cementing the close relationship that continues today[1]

Several huge construction projects backed by the Soviet bloc represent the investment of hundreds of millions of dollars, including $70 million for nearly 40 new military facilities. In addition, Bulgaria, East Germany, and Cuba are building critical infrastructure facilities which will have important military uses.

The 10,000-foot runway at the Punta Huete airfield, when completed, will be the longest military runway in Central America. As the base took on the unmistakable signs of a military air base, such as protective earthen mounds (or revetments) for fighter aircraft, the Sandinista Air Force Commander admitted that it would be a military air base.

When Punta Heute becomes operational, it will be able to accommodate any aircraft in the Soviet-bloc inventory, to include the long-range BEAR-D reconnaissance aircraft.

Soviet-made helicopters, listed as "crop dusters" have been delivered to the Sandinistas. The recent acquisition of 12-24 Soviet Mi-24/HIND D attack helicopters, called "*The Flying Tank*", provides the Nicaraguan government with air-

State Department photo

Soviet "Flying Tank"
MI-24/HIND-D attack helicopter

to-air, air-to-ground missiles, night radar and other sophisticated equipment. At the present time there is nothing in the US inventory to match this aircraft. Along with the existing inventory of Mi-8 troop-carrying helicopters, it provides the Sandinistas with a powerful force.[2]

The regime in Nicaragua poses both a real and psychological threat to the countries of Central America. This fact is readily perceived by the citizens of Nicaragua's neighboring countries as was revealed in a public opinion poll conducted by Gallup International in 1983.

This poll showed that Nicaragua's growing military strength and support for subversive movements in other countries was a source of concern throughout the region. In Honduras, for example, about 80 percent of the respondents saw Nicaragua as the principal cause of instability and as the primary military threat faced by their country.[3]

RELIGIOUS PERSECUTION IN NICARAGUA

Perhaps the most tragic persecution has been inflicted on the indians of Nicaragua's isolated Atlantic coast. Most of the members of the Miskito, Sumo, and Rama tribes are members of minority Protestant churches, especially the Moravian Church.

A White House report explains: "When the Sandinistas came to power in 1979, they immediately announced that their top priority was to 'rescue the Atlantic Coast.' Cuban and Nicaraguan personnel began to flood in . . . they sealed off the area. Travel to the region was allowed only by special permit. Indians were drafted into the militia. Those who refused were shot or forcibly relocated. Villages were forcibly evacuated and then burned . . . the Sandinistas destroyed Moravian Churches."[4]

The White House Report continues: "In November 1982, the Misurasata Council of Ancients (elders), the legitimate representatives of the people of the three tribes, officially denounced the Sandinista government before the OAS. They said, 'their people had suffered lack of respect for our religious beliefs and traditions, imprisonment of our leaders, massive captures of peasants, women, the aged and children, rapes, beatings, torture, and the death and disappearance of prisoners . . .'

The details are particularly horrifying: "In January and February of 1982, the FSLN *destroyed 49 communities, burned more than 4,000 houses*, and then, so that no one could return to their land of origin, cut down fruit trees, *shot all the domestic animals . . . and forced the residents to march 11 to 15 days to different concentration camps.*"

During the forced march . . . *the invalids, lame, blind and paralyzed persons* were gathered together in the village of Tulinbilia, *[where] they were put inside the church and they were burned*—13 persons thus died."

The overwhelming evidence of the wide-spread persecution of Christian churches in Nicaragua is a sad reminder of the sometimes forgotten nature of Marxism-Leninism, and its total hatred and disregard for freedom of religion.

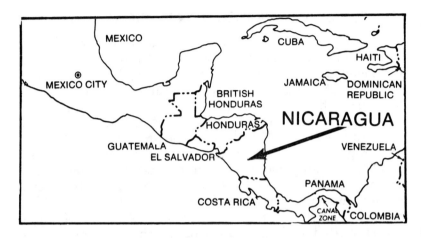

NICARAGUA THREAT

Panama played a key role in providing military support to the Sandinistas in 1978 and 1979. After the Sandinistas came to power, however, they rejected Panama's advice and offers of assistance. Recently, General Manuel Noriega, Commander of Panama's Defense Force, told editors of Costa Rica's principal newspaper, *La Nacion*, that Sandinista arms escalation posed a danger to the entire region.

In the article in *La Nacion* reporting Noriega's view, the editors wrote that "**Sandinista militarism has to be halted before it produces a holocaust in the entire Caribbean region.**"[5]

Honduras shares a 570-mile border with Nicaragua. The Sandinistas have conducted training with tanks, armored personnel carriers, and long-range artillery in areas close to the Choluteca Gap. The Honduran army is striving to modernize and professionalize, but it lags behind the rapid expansion of the Sandinista army. Costa Rica has no army. The Salvadoran armed forces are fully occupied with combating Sandinista-supported insurgents. Clearly, Nicaragua's military power threatens—and is not threatened by—its neighbors.[6]

Chapter 17

Grenada: Communism Halted

What happened in Grenada? How did a Marxist-Leninist revolution begin?

Grenada turned toward the Cubans and the Soviet bloc in 1979, when Maurice Bishop led a coup to depose the unpopular Prime Minister, Eric Gairy. Bishop promised that his revolution would modernize the economy, improve living standards, and promote democracy.[1]

Secretly Bishop planned to impose a dictatorship while promising pluralistic democracy. His *New Jewel Movement* (NJM) was organized along classic Marxist-Leninist lines, with power concentrated in a single leader and exercised through a small central committee. The NJM was led by the radical left, but it also included non-Communist elements.

"This was done," Bishop explained in his speech on 13 September 1982, "*so Imperialism won't get too excited.*"[2]

Later, he removed the moderates from government, as Castro had done 20 years before in Cuba. Elections were never held. Opposition was dealt with firmly, often through imprisonment. The media was controlled. "The so-called *"People's Laws"* gave Bishop and his top lieutenants nearly unlimited power. Children and adults were required to attend political indoctrination classes. In many respects, Bishop was repeating the steps taken by Castro in the early 1960's.

State Department photo

ORTEGA   BISHOP   CASTRO

Photo at NJM political meeting shows Daniel Ortega, Maurice Bishop, and Fidel Castro.

Bishop called his regime the *People's Revolutionary Government* and established close ties with the Soviet Union, Cuba, and to a lesser extent, Libya, North Korea, and Vietnam. The extent of Soviet-Grenadian relations was not made known until after Bishop visited Moscow in July 1982, and even then key details were kept from the public.

Only a month after Bishop seized power, the first large shipment of arms arrived from Havana. This included 3,400 rifles, 200 machine guns, 100 heavier weapons, and ammunition. Hundreds of young Grenadians were sent to Cuba for military training. The Grenadian Army Chief of Staff and both of Grenada's Secretaries of Defense went to the USSR for training.

In a 15 April 1983 meeting with Grenadian Prime Minister Maurice Bishop, Soviet Foreign Minister Andrei Gromyko was quoted as describing the region as *"boiling like a*

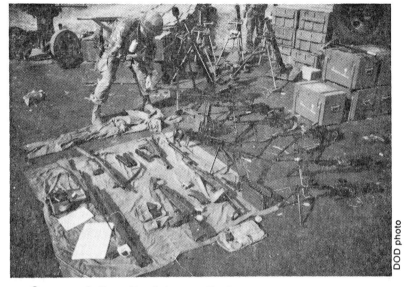

DOD photo

**Some of the Soviet-supplied weapons found in
Grenadian warehouses.**

cauldron," and saw Cuba and Nicaragua as "living examples
for countries in that part of the world."

Cautious opportunism was evident in Gromyko's words,
advising Bishop that **"Imperialism should not be agitated
. . . to avoid alerting the United States prematurely."** At the
same time he urged Grenada to continue revolutionary
operations in the region.[3]

The Point Salines airport project was a key issue for
Maurice Bishop in his 15 April 1983 meeting with Andrei
Gromyko . . . he emphasized the economic benefits of the
project, but also pointed out, "the strategic factor is well
known!!" The Point Salinas airfield was scheduled to be
inaugurated on 13 March 1984. Its runway length (10,000
feet), would have enabled it to serve as a stopover point for
Cuban and Soviet aircraft.[4]

Once completed, Point Salines could have provided a
stopover point for Cuban flights to Africa, an additional

facility for Soviet long-range reconnaissance aircraft, and possibly a transshipment point for arms and supplies for Latin American insurgents.

Had the Point Salines airport been operational in April 1983, for example, the Libyan aircraft detained in Brazil, clandestinely ferrying a cargo of military supplies for Nicaragua, could have refueled in Grenada instead of Brazil.

To further Grenada's regional ambitions, the Bishop government adopted an active program of meeting with *"progressive and revolutionary parties in the region"* twice a year to heat up Gromyko's "boiling cauldron." Soviet interest in exploiting the problems of Central America and the Caribbean is evident in a document found by US-Caribbean security forces during the Grenada rescue mission.

Belize and *Suriname* were seen as particularly ripe for exploitation.

In July 1983, the Grenadian Ambassador to Moscow sent a message to his Foreign Minister emphasizing the continuing need "For Grenada to assume a position of increasingly greater importance . . . we have to establish ourselves as . . . the sponsor of revolutionary activity and progressive developments in this region at least."[5]

By October 1983, tiny Grenada had more men under arms and more weapons and military supplies than all of its Eastern Caribbean neighbors combined—with plans to give Grenada one of the largest military forces in proportion to population of any country in the world.

A power struggle erupted with the New Jewel Movement during the fall of 1983. Bishop was assassinated, along with three of his closest deputies, and the killing of scores of innocent persons by troops of the *People's Revolutionary Army*, which led to the collapse of the NJM.

All ports of entry and departure were closed and a 24-hour shoot-on-sight curfew was declared.

In the fall of 1983, the Organization of Eastern Caribbean States made a formal request to the United States for assistance. In addition, the sole remaining source of governmental legitimacy, the Governor-General of Grenada, Sir

State Department photo

Grenadian soldiers marching. The New Jewel Movement had militarized Grenadian society in the classic pattern of a Marxist-Leninist dictatorship.

Paul Scoon, made an urgent and confidential appeal to the regional states to restore order on the island.

The United States, responding to these requests and concern over the safety of 1,000 American citizens on the island, participated in a combined US-Caribbean security force that landed on Grenada on 25 October 1983. Peace and public order were restored.

The reaction of the Grenadian people to the US and Carribbean security force was overwhelmingly supportive. A CBS News poll of 3 November 1983 found that 91 percent of the Grenadian people expressed strong approval for the actions taken by the United States.

In spite of four years of Marxist-Leninist indoctrination by the Bishop regime, the people of Grenada welcomed the US-Caribbean troops as liberators.

On 3 December 1984, the people of Grenada formally closed the books on the failed Marxist-Leninist revolution by successfully holding the island's first election in eight years.

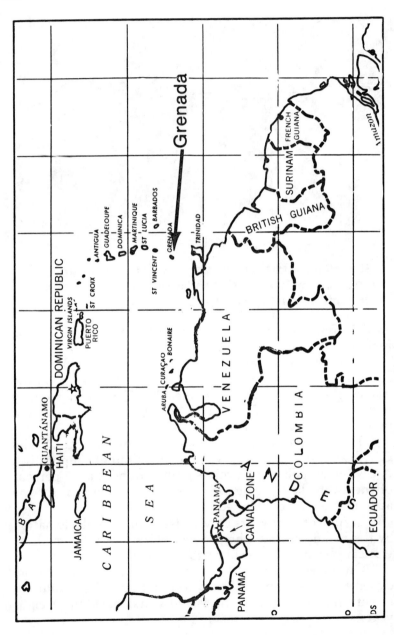

Chapter 18

Mexico:
Communism Closer To Home

Few Americans are aware of what is happening in Mexico, but it is time we who are Christians in America woke up to the developments there. A recent report alerted us to the serious trouble stirring south of our border.[1]

It is almost impossible to purchase American goods in Mexico. They have been outlawed! All American companies have been partially or entirely nationalized. Foreign investment is discouraged and in many industries forbidden. The government policies have brought about poverty. It is a hopeless economy, due to inflation, taxation and negative investment incentives, despite tremendous natural resources.

The Mexican people have no confidence in their government. They do not turn to the police for protection, because the police prey upon them. The Communists are the only significant opposition to the ruling Socialist Party, promising a new government free from corruption. Freedom from corruption appeals to the people, who have been oppressed by corrupt government as long as they can remember.

The poverty is a striking contrast to America. The typical family spends every bit of their energy eking out a living. Tiny boys hawk wares on the streets. Vendors and little shops are everywhere, as each family member does what he must to live. Despite the poverty, families look for every excuse to have celebrations and family get-togethers have a

festive air. Despite Socialism and Communism there is more
private enterprise in Mexico than in America.

MEXICAN GOVERNMENT CATERS TO SOVIETS

The current government in Mexico is just short of
Soviet Communism. Many prominent, high level government officials are committed Communists who hope to align
Mexico with the Soviet Union. *Koinonia* reports: Mexico and
the USSR are already firm allies. Mexico City and many U.S.
border towns are well known bases for Soviet spy activity in
America.

Mexico officially caters to the Soviets and the Cubans in
international affairs . . . and has been particularly prominent
in supporting the Sandinista government in Nicaragua.

MEXICO—RIPE FOR REVOLUTION

All major services for the people are owned and operated by the national or state government: telephone services, banks, oil companies, utilities, gas, refineries and dis-
tributors, etc. Gasoline prices are controlled at 55 pesos per
liter throughout the country. The poor can obtain subsid-
ized government bread almost free of charge in local markets.

The Mexican federal government, through its control of
the currency, plunders its people. Inflation is officially 55
percent per year, but natives say it is really nearer 100 percent. There have been several significant official devalua-
tions of the currency during the past few years. Upper middle class people earn around $400 per month. Common
people do much worse. Federal income taxes for the average
man are 25 percent and a national sales tax of 15 percent is
charged on all manufactured or processed goods.

According to *Koinonia*, literally "all" government officials
are corrupt. With few exceptions, the police are crooked by
American standards and taking of bribes is *the norm*. The
people, who have been raped by the prevailing political party
(PRI), are ripe for a change. There is talk of revolution

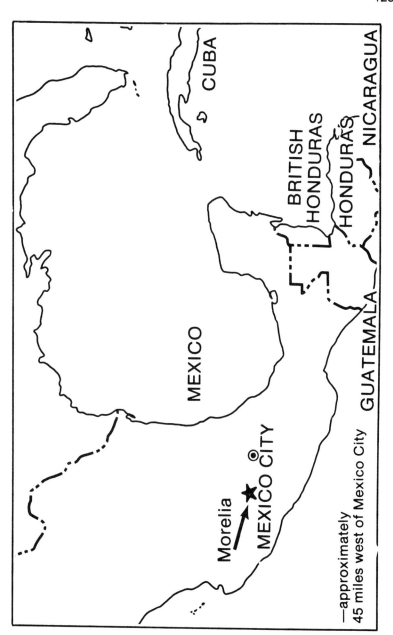

CUBA

BRITISH
HONDURAS

HONDURAS

NICARAGUA

MEXICO

GUATEMALA

MEXICO CITY

Morelia

—approximately
45 miles west of Mexico City

throughout Mexico, but particularly in Morelia, which is a kind of headquarters for Communism in the country.

In May 1985, in the city of Morelia, there were Communist rallies in the city streets. They consisted of loud protests against the present government and chanting pro-communist slogans. Poor laborers really had little understanding of what they were doing, but were simply responding to very effective organization and regimentation. The organizers appear to be college age or slightly older but cried out with a zeal and fire that was extremely impressive.

MORELIA-HEADQUARTERS FOR COMMUNISM

Several huge colleges, teachers' schools, and a state university are located in Morelia (the capital city of the state of Michuoacan). Here Soviet and Cuban trained teachers and administrators indoctrinate Mexican students in Communist ideology.

At a highly esteemed teacher training college between Morelia and Uruapan, public school teachers and administrators are *"retrained"* from year to year to asssure a growing commitment to Communism among the youth. In 1985, Cuba provided Michuoacan 500 "retrainers" to teach in the colleges and to be placed in principal positions in the local schools.

All student textbooks in Michuoacan were reported to be stamped with the hammer and sickle in 1985.

The block walls of the teachers' college between Morelia and Uruapan are covered with Communist, revolutionary, and **Anti-American** slogans and catchwords. **The hammer and sickle are displayed everywhere** . . . and people, particularly the church leaders, are afraid to say anything against Communism.

Conversation with an average man or woman on the street in Mexico does not indicate that Mexicans fear Communism. Like Americans who know little or nothing about Humanism and its power, Mexicans know little about Communism and its threat to them. Every family member of the typical family spends every bit of energy eking out a living. They don't have time for "politics." To them Communism is just another political ideology that can't be any worse than they've had in the past.

It is simply **assumed** that Communism will obtain full control of the country within the next three years, either peacefully or by revolutionary means. It seems the only potential opponent to a Communist takeover is the church.

RELIGION IN MEXICO

Catholicism in Mexico is practiced differently than in America. Every town has its own "Virgin" who is worshipped by all the townspeople. At least once a year pilgrimages are made by the faithful on special days to honor their hometown Virgin. Some walk for miles, falling on their knees to crawl the last few miles as they humble themselves before their Virgin. Each pilgrim prays she will grant them some special favor.

The festival of the *"Virgin of Guadelupe"* is the biggest annual event in Mexico. This Virgin, the patron saint of Mexico, is said to have had a vision of Jesus and Mary walking. People report miracles are performed in her name and by her power. Everything, including government, closes down to observe her day.

Cathedrals dominate the towns and tower over all other buildings. The people are devoted to the church and the church building. Inside there are statues of Mary and other brightly clad virgins. Statues of the dead or dying Christ are outnumbered by virgins three or four to one. Some cathedrals have glass cabinets containing life-like figures of Christ, lying "in state."

The government is increasing control over religion in Mexico. Churches may purchase property, but upon building any structure must deed the property to the states. The church may continue to use the property as long as the government wishes. If the government needs the property for any secular purpose, it may confiscate it at will. The church is in jeopardy if it begins to preach or teach anything that would threaten those in power.

The Catholics and the Communists have compromised with one another philosophically, and join together in their opposition toward evangelicals, who number less than 5 percent. Evangelicals (called *Alleluiahs* by the common people), particularly the missionaries, are regularly accused of being capitalists, and CIA agents who are trying to turn Mexico away from her cherished values and strengths (Catholicism).

Witchcraft thrives in Mexico. Street vendors hawk their potions, cures, spells and blessings for a price. Voo-doo dolls can be purchased in the open markets.

Some witches have brought their practice into the churches themselves. Female witches, and sometimes male witches, cast curses on the churches and their members—striking fear into the hearts of even the church leaders. Because of superstition and fear, many folks will not even visit an evangelical church. Some witches have a following that exceeds the membership of the evangelical churches.

Doors for evangelism are almost closed. Unless Mexican and American Christians begin intense intercession for God's mercy, there is little hope that Mexico will be saved from the grip of Communism.

Fifty percent of the Mexican population is under 15 years old, and another fifteen to twenty percent is under 25.

Dedicated Communists compose only a tiny percent of the populace, but are impacting significantly beyond their number. **This gives hope**. If they can do it, Christians can do the same!

Chapter 19

Moral Aspects of Deterrence

In a speech given by Secretary of Defense, Caspar Weinberger, in April 1983, at Fordham University in New York City, he spoke of Moses' appeal to God's people:

' ". . . I set before you life or death, blessing or curse. *Choose life*, then, so that you and your descendants may live.' "

". . . religious leaders today call us, not just as men and women responsible for our individual souls, but as a nation responsible for our common fate, to *choose life* . . . you will not hear me talk today about rendering unto Caesar—for life is a gift, not of Caesar, but of God."

"The charge to choose life is also a political responsibility, echoed in our *Declaration of Independence* and in our *Constitution*. And in the age of nuclear weapons this charge has taken on new meaning for all people . . . because now a nation truly can choose between life and death—between peace with freedom, or a *peace such as Poland endures, without freedom*, and it chooses not just for itself but for its descendants."

Secretary Weinberger continued, "*our constitutional responsibility 'to provide for the common defense' is an awesome one*. It poses terrible questions and imposes terrible burdens . . . with no margin for error."

". . . in speaking today about moral and religious dimensions to nuclear deterrence, I intend to speak from two perspectives: that of an individual Christian, and that of the Secretary of Defense . . . I have been forced to confront (these challenges), so also will each one of you . . ."

"Consider, for example, the Biblical injunction to love your enemy. The individual Christian is called to turn the other cheek . . . *yet a Christian acting on behalf of his nation*, or, in the case of the United States, on behalf of an alliance of free nations, *cannot simply turn the cheek of innocent people toward their aggressors*, or hand over the fruits of other peoples' labor."

"By the end of World War II, we found ourselves . . . the richest and most powerful nation in the world—and in sole possession of the most terrible weapons mankind has ever known. With our monopoly on nuclear weapons, the United States *sought not* to control the world, but, through the Baruch Plan, *to put those weapons under international control*. With our material wealth the United States sought *not* to establish an empire, but to rebuild democracy and *rekindle economic growth for friend and foe alike*. We tried, I believe harder than any nation has tried before, to *love those who had been enemies*, to 'seek peace and pursue it.' Psalm 34:14."

Secretary Weinberger reminded his audience, "In seeking peace, we pursued a strategy of deterrence that has been the basis of our defense policy ever since George Washington . . . (who) in the very first State of the Union address, told Congress: *"to be prepared for war is one of the most effectual means of preserving peace."*

". . . three challenges we must keep before us, as we debate the morality of war and peace in the nuclear age:

"First is the horror of *all* wars. We must seek to prevent not just another Hiroshima, but also another Dresden, or Bataan. When fifty million people died in World War II, it was a lesson for all time that *holocaust need not be nuclear*—we must protect us all from the awesome conventional power of the Soviet Union—a power the Soviets have shown in Hungary, in Czechoslovakia, and in Afghanistan that they are willing to use. A power demonstrated in the use of chemical and toxin weapons in violation of their treaty obligations, against soldiers and civilians alike."

". . . another challenge of the nuclear age . . . the United States rejects a strategy which targets nuclear weapons against population centers. But to maintain a credible deterrent we must be able to retaliate against military targets . . . for this we need very modern and accurate weapons."

Secretary Weinberger also reflected "a concern which President Reagan raised in his recent speech to the American people. 'Would it not, he asked, be better to save lives than to avenge them? His answer was to propose that week to develop a new defense against nuclear missiles.' "

"The third challenge: The behavior of the Soviet Union—a regime which explicitly *rejects* the laws and the love of God. During the 1970's the United States made a conscious choice to restrict its nuclear weapons developments so that the Soviet Union would not feel we had a first strike threat, and therefore, first strike intentions."

"But the Soviets did not follow our *self-imposed restraint*. Instead, they developed several new ICBM's specifically designed to destroy U.S. missile silos and B-52 bases. And they continue to deploy a vast array of *additional* weapons to threaten us and our allies . . . their writings, military doctrine, and exercises emphasize the kind of nuclear warfighting scen-rio which we, in the United States, have rejected—and which we must deter."

". . . I believe that religion and morality call us to judge between good and evil."

Concluding, the Secretary said, "Let us not lose confidence that America has a special mission for peace. **Our Constitution calls us to . . . 'secure the blessings of liberty for ourselves and our posterity.'** Our leadership in the free world calls us to help our friends and allies deter aggression . . ."

"Our strategy of deterrence, then, is a strategy for . . . *peace with liberty*, with justice, and *with the freedom to follow the dictates of God*, and our conscience. To choose less is *not* to choose life, in the true and full sense of that great blessing."

Chapter 20

Why Has God Allowed It?

Why has God allowed our enemies to triumph over America? There are many reasons. Isaiah the prophet warns us:

> **"The nation that will not serve God shall perish and be destroyed."** Isaiah 60:12

In Iran our Embassy personnel were taken as hostages, our Embassy taken over by mobs and the American flag burned. America seemed powerless to rescue the hostages. Our one daring attempt to do so was foiled by a mighty sand storm which caused our helicopters to crash.

Our peace-keeping mission to Beirut ended in humiliation and much loss of life. How could God allow our efforts to keep a small nation from being overrun by Syria to fail? Our brave marines on the beach were no match for the Syrian forces lobbing shells down from their fortresses in the mountains. The truck bomb attack on our Marine headquarters was unbelievable. Americans watched and cried, but seemed powerless to do anything against the terrorists. Finally our troops were withdrawn—and Syria moved in. We failed miserably.

Increasing terrorist attacks, such as the bombing of the U.S. Capitol building, and the U.S. Navy Yard in Washington, DC have caused Americans to take a good look at defending our leaders and historic buildings. Concrete barriers and barricades have been erected around the White House, Capitol, State Department and Pentagon. But they are no match for a terrorist who is willing to give his life while blowing up a building!

Why has God allowed America to become weak, when once we were strong? **Why?**

Americans have made idols in their hearts. Idols of activities which they *know* are immoral, but they refuse to give up. They say: "God doesn't see—it's nobody's business what I do in my own home. The Bible is out of date—everyone is doing this." Idols can be anything that takes more of our time—even our thinking time—than we give to God.

God says: ". . . Thus saith the Lord God: **repent**, and turn yourselves from your idols; and turn away your faces from all your abominations." Ezekiel 14:1-6

Reason 1. **SPORTS**

Sports figures are idolized and set up as role models for Americans. Many Americans spend six hours a day watching sports on television. It has become a god to some who forsake all to attend Superbowls and championship events.

Reason 2. **MAKING MONEY**

Money, career, and prestige have become a time and energy consuming god.

Reason 3. **PLEASURE SEEKING**

Expensive vacations and search for constant entertainment. Each has become a god.

Reason 4. **FOOD**

Increased consumption of fast foods and sweets, obsession with menus, new recipes, and gourmet delights has brought on poor health.

Reason 5. **PERSONALITIES**

Americans idolize people in entertainment, sports and other fields—including religious leaders.

Reason 6. **OUR JOBS**
Being successful has become a number one priority. Many spend most waking hours away from family pursuing a career, with little time for God.

Reason 7. **OUR HOMES**
The effort required to maintain a beautifully landscaped yard or having the biggest home, better than anyone else's, has made our homes an idol.

Reason 8. **TELEVISION**
More time is spent in front of the tube than any other activity. Many Christians admit they spend an average of 6 hours a day viewing their favorite shows.

Reason 9. **HOBBIES**
America's hobbies are expensive and time consuming. Collecting antiques, coins, dolls, guns, stamps or pumping iron takes time away from God.

Anything that takes more of our thinking time, more of our leisure time, more of our money, than we spend on God—has become an idol. God says **repent!**
Idolatry and perversion caused the downfall of the Roman Empire. It was the greatest known power in the world—until it began to deteriorate in its morals—and it fell. Like the Roman Empire, the immorality in America is destroying our strength. Contrary to what politicians think, we will *never* achieve economic power, nor military power, nor security until we clean up our morals.
- **ABORTION**
Since the infamous *Roe vs Wade* decision in 1973 by the Supreme Court, America has suffered increased humiliation and defeat. The killing of an unborn baby is now called the "removal of fetal tissue" or "discontinuing of pregnancy."
In California, 14,000 fetuses were discovered. Photographs revealed these tiny unborn infants were preserved, stored in jars filled with formaldehyde. Some of the larger

babies had been decapitated because their bodies would not fit into the jar.

Each of these jars contained the results of an abortion—murder demanded as a "right" of the mother, to do as she pleased with this unborn baby. In California Christians sought to have these remains buried, to give dignity to these unborns. But a California judge ruled that they were not human remains and forbade burial! The court did not have to prove that they were animal, vegetable, mineral, OR human. They simply declared they would be incinerated—disposed of as garbage.

Many of the abortion chambers where 15 million unborn babies have been murdered are considered **charitable institutions**, by the Internal Revenue Service and are tax-exempt! We must repent!

• HOMOSEXUALITY

Homosexuality is being taught in public school health classes across America as "normal." The courts have ruled that homosexual teachers must be allowed to teach your children. TV films show homosexuals in a favorable light. In many states courts have ruled that landlords cannot refuse to rent to homosexual couples. God calls it sin!

• PORNOGRAPHY—TV, MOVIES, MAGAZINES

Los Angeles, New York and Cleveland are distribution centers for pornography and the government isn't doing anything except for kiddie-porn, which only acounts for 1 percent of the pornography business in this country, according to William Kelley, former Chief of the FBI. The Mafia is involved—the god of pornography is money.

According to the results of a Gallup Poll in 1985, 13 percent of the religious leaders, 50 percent of the educators, 46 percent of the military, 53 percent of the government leaders, and 54 percent of the media think that **pornography isn't a moral issue!** They say, "If you don't like pornography, don't read it."

In 1984, 81 percent of the sex killers testified that they

had indulged in masturbation while reading or watching pornography shortly before attacking their victim. Yet, *Playboy* and *Hustler* are tolerated as "harmless."

• DRUGS AND ALCOHOL

Beer is used favorably by sports figures and alcoholic drinks by stars on America's TV, and now alcoholism is more rampant than drugs. Drugs are sold on school grounds and on streets of our nation in broad daylight. We are playing right into satan's hand—destroying our youth.

• OCCULT INVOLVEMENT

Occult cartoons, board games and video games feature Dungeons and Dragons, evil Masters of the Universe, wizards, witches, spells and omens to lure America's children into occult deception. Witchcraft and magic are themes for commercials and TV programs. Deception, deceit, and darkness are becoming acceptable themes.

☆   GOD OFFERS A SOLUTION   ☆

"At what instant I shall speak concerning a nation, and concerning a kingdom, to pluck up, and to pull down, and to destroy it—If that nation, against whom I have pronounced, turn from their evil, I will repent of the evil that I thought to do unto them." Jeremiah 18:7-8

America, Wake Up! Repent and turn again to God.

The time is now, not tomorrow, to pray for America. God is looking for intercessors who "should make up the hedge, and stand in the gap, before Him, *for the land*—that he should not destroy it . . ." Ezekiel 22:30

If we will meet His conditions, God will relent, and heal our land:

"If my people, which are called by my name, shall humble themselves and pray, and seek my face and turn from their wicked ways, then will I hear from heaven and will forgive their sin and will heal their land."

II Chronicles 7:14

America must roll up its sleeves and face the Communist danger.

Chapter 21

In Debt, Dissatisfied and Discontent

How long has it been since you read the Declaration of Independence? Perhaps it is time to review it again. It reads as follows:

"We hold these truths to be self evident, that all men are created equal; that they are endowed by their *creator* with certain unalienable rights, that among these are life, liberty, and the pursuit of happiness. That, to secure these rights, governments are instituted among men, deriving their just powers from the *consent of the governed*; that, whenever any form of government becomes destructive to these ends, it is the right of the people to alter or to abolish it, and to institute a new government, laying its foundations on such principles, and organizing its powers in such form, as to them shall seem most likely to effect their safety and happiness."

Vice President George Bush reminded the thousands of Americans gathered at Constitution Hall, in Washington, DC in 1984, for the National Day of Prayer, "Today it can truthfully be said—merely to be an American is to be blessed."

There are powerful forces at work here in America to turn us into a Socialist-Marxist type of government—taking away the rights of individuals, families, and our free enterprise work ethic.

- Thomas Jefferson said, "God, who gave us life, gave us liberty."
- Lenin said, "Liberty is so precious it must be rationed to only a few." According to Lenin, liberty should be rationed only to the Communists—those who have grabbed the freedoms of other countries around the world.

Freedoms we take for granted in America are *totally forbidden* in Communist countries:

- **FREEDOM OF SPEECH**—dissidents are jailed, hospitalized or disappear.
- **FREEDOM OF TRAVEL**—can't go anywhere without permission.
- **FREEDOM OF RELIGION**—four churches in Moscow are approved to hold services for over two million people who live in the area. It is against the law to teach young people, no Sunday Schools. No meetings in homes. No meetings may be held unless approved by the government.
- **FREEDOM TO BE EDUCATED**—only the elite members of the Communist party are chosen.
- **FREEDOM TO CHOOSE YOUR VOCATION**—women are given equal pay and equal work with no special treatment—they do street cleaning and repair roads. The government decides on wages based on workers' needs, not ability or worth.
- **FREE ENTERPRISE SYSTEM**—can't start or own a private business.
- **FREEDOM TO RUN FOR POLITICAL OFFICE**—only one party, one name on ballot, can only vote if you are a Communist member in good standing.
- **FREEDOM TO BEAR ARMS**—no weapons to defend yourself against invasion of your home by the KGB or anyone else.
- **FREEDOM TO OWN PRIVATE PROPERTY**—the government owns everything. You are assigned where to live, paid a government-set wage. Food, clothing,

and furniture are in short supply or rationed—people stand in long lines for available items.

- **FREEDOM OF FAMILIES**—in eastern Europe the home is under ruthless attack by the Communist authorities. Karl Marx even went so far as to call marriage "private prostitution!"

  In the eyes of atheistic governments, children are property of the state. Parents should have little or no influence on them. Children are educated, selected for athletic or military training, university or a job— whichever the government decides.

Do you see the freedoms we could lose? These liberties must not be taken for granted. Freedom is constantly attacked by those who would like to deny it to us! It is denied to most people in the world.

"THE PRICE OF LIBERTY IS THE ABILITY TO DEFEND AND PRESERVE IT."

The bottom line on defense issues is simple . . . to protect and preserve the American way of life and the God-given freedoms that we must richly cherish. We must be alert and ever ready to defend our nation against enemies both from within and without our borders.

President Teddy Roosevelt said it well, "We must speak softly, but carry a big stick."

Those who speak loudly for disarmament are playing right into the hands of the Communists. The Soviets have never kept any agreement they have signed—do we naively think they would keep any treaty in the future? The supporters the Communists find most valuable now would be eliminated when the Soviets take control. The radicals who speak out loudly now must be silenced later—under Marxism.

HOOVER'S WARNING

J. Edgar Hoover, former Chief of the FBI, warned that it

was easy to become a member of the Communist Party. They are always looking for new members. They look for any *discontent, disatisfaction, rebellion against authority, racial unrest, student uprisings or strikers.* They fan the flame and add fuel to the fire.

You can become a pawn, a useful tool for the Communists—without joining the party. Their eyes and ears are open for recruits. They look for:

1. Military or government personnel who could obtain valuable information for them through their jobs.
2. They are always on the lookout for people at public events and places such as bars.
3. They look for people who drink too much and might need some extra cash to support their expensive tastes.
4. They look for men who might be lonely and desire a beautiful girlfriend.
5. They look for closet homosexuals.
6. They look for anyone who has a government job or access to classified information.

These people are open to blackmail, bribes, and exposure. If you are a loner, or lonely—the Communists could supply you with a date, or a mate. If you are black and have strong racial feelings, they could supply you with an attractive white person to date. If you have a secret lust problem, you could be offered a sex partner. This is a common tactic. Communists look for your weakness.

The Communists don't ask for anything—at first. But once you are ensnared they bribe, threaten to reveal your traitorous acts, and if that isn't enough they will threaten to kill your family.

You must be wary of any contacts with foreigners—even if they claim to be from a non-Communist country. Report any request for information, phone books, papers, documents or manuals, even if they are unclassified.

Remember, anyone can be a Communist. Movie stars, Congressmen, ministers or priests, university professors, students, rock stars, sports figures, newscasters, school board members, school teachers, state and federal government officials, artists, musicians—neither ordinary people nor celebrities are immune to their wiles.

Today our media is very pro-communist. Communism is shown in a favorable light. Americans are often confused by terms used on the nightly news—terms and words which are constantly changing. A few key words to look for:

Independent Party, Fighters for Democracy, Sandinistas, insurgents, Leftists, Agrarian Reformers, People's Party, Nationalists, Marxists, Socialists—all are Communists.

If you are in debt, dissatisfied, discontent, or have a desire for power—you could be a candidate for Communism.

We must be aware of our enemy's tactics.

Chapter 22

Understanding the Times

We've considered the Communists and the terrorists because they are a constant threat to our nation's peace and security, but the real enemy behind atheistic Communism is the enemy of all mankind—**satan**.

Why is satan seeking to destroy America?

Because, in spite of our sinfulness, America is fulfilling the Great Commission—to carry the gospel into all the world. America has always been concerned with evangelism of those who have never heard the good news in other lands, and also with Bible translation into the languages of tribes who have never learned to read or write in their own tongues.

A look at a world map would reveal that America is only a tiny fraction of the total land mass. Yet our nation does more than all other nations in the world combined to fund missionaries and Bible translation work. Over ninety percent of all the funds for worldwide missions and Bible translation come from the USA.

In addition to giving enormous amounts of money for the work of the gospel, the United States provides the most missionary personnel, Bible translation teams, and backup support staff—about ninety percent of the total worldwide missionary workers. Americans are concerned enough to go themselves or to train and fund others who are willing to do the work Jesus commissioned—taking the gospel into all the world.

America has responded to the scriptural command to

feed the hungry, clothe the naked, and care for the aged, as well as those who are sick or in prison. Our nation responds quickly to disasters anywhere in the world by sending emergency relief teams, food, clothing, tents, medicine and money to assist in rebuilding the stricken area. America has had a caring heart—concern for people in need worldwide.

Following World War II, America followed the Biblical command to love your enemies by giving huge amounts of foreign aid and outright grants to rebuild Japan and Germany—even though these nations had inflicted heavy loss of American life.

Is it any wonder that God has blessed our nation?

Jerry Lee Lewis voices our sentiments, "I'm so glad I'm livin' in the USA"!

America was conceived in liberty—are we going to defend it and pass it on? If so, we must remember those who gave their lives that we might enjoy the blessings of liberty—those who made the supreme sacrifice to preserve freedom.

Senator Jeremiah Denton (R/Alabama), who was held captive in North Viet Nam for seven years and, as the highest ranking officer, was the most tortured prisoner of war, spoke at Arlington Cemetary, near the Tomb of the Unknown Soldier on Memorial Day 1985. He reminded us that:

"The nation that forgets its defenders will itself be forgotten."

America is not perfect. But America is the free-est nation in the world. The key to America remaining free lies in the hands of Christians!

Too often Christians have withdrawn from politics, from education, from social issues, and are just waiting around for the rapture! With this kind of mentality it's no wonder that Christians have little effect on world opinion or events.

According to a U.S. News and World Report poll taken in 1984 which rated forces influencing American thinking, the church ranked #29 out of 30. And in 1985 the poll was worse. Church was rated **last**! Having the least influence in the lives of Americans!

Christians have said: "One person can't make any difference. I don't want to get involved in all these worldly issues, I'm just going to wait for the Lord's return."

But Lenin said: "I'll change the world!" He set out to do it and he did.

We often think, what can I do? I'm only one person. But everyone can make a difference. We've got to stop blaming others and stop living our lives to please ourselves. Instead we must commit our lives to God and turn our nation around for Jesus Christ, decency, and morality.

We each have a decision to make about America's future, and our own. We can—we must—get involved if we're going to get back to our biblical foundation. We must humble ourselves, repent of our apathy and prayerlessness, and ask God to use us, and help us change our nation.

"All it takes for evil to triumph is for good men to do nothing." A few ways you can get involved are:

- In the very important elections held every year— elections which affect your nation, your state, your county, and the city in which you live.
- It is the duty of every Christian to be informed and to vote. It takes time to read and to study the local, state and national issues carefully. Then we must spend time in prayer and fasting to seek God's guidance on voting decisions.
- Work at the local precinct, and in your political party, to elect godly candidates to office. Attend your county and state political conventions, volunteer to be a delegate, volunteer to go door to door with literature—in order to inform your neighbors on issues.
- Very important legislation is considered almost daily on Capitol Hill—legislation which will affect you, your job, your finances, your local schools, your family, your grandchildren, your future. Liberals are lobbying for their views. Christian voices must be heard!
- It is the duty of every Christian to be informed. It takes time to read Christian newsletters and reports, but these keep us informed.

- It is the duty of Christians to speak out on issues. Inform others in your churches, civic and community groups. The conservative voice must be heard, not just the liberal demanding his "rights."
- We must insist on a balanced budget for the federal government. Runaway give-away federal programs have almost totally bankrupted our nation. The income from taxes paid by every citizen in 42 states was spent in 1985 to pay the **interest** on the national debt, according to Senator Bill Armstrong!
- It is the duty of every Christian to write to his legislators. Take time to visit the offices of your Senators and Congressmen—it takes time and energy but we must fight to re-establish morality in America.
- It is the duty of Christians to pray. The time is now, not tomorrow, to pray for America. We are commanded to pray for all in authority over us, in order that we might lead a quiet and peaceable life in all godliness. I Tim 2:1-2

    God is calling forth men and women who will stand in the gap, and make up the hedge for our nation, so that HE will not destroy it. Become an intercessor—a prayer warrior. It takes time. Many elderly saints feel they have lost their usefulness; but they can take up this call to arms!

God is calling forth men and women in the church who:
- Understand the times.
- Know what the church is called to do—be salt and light.
- Know how to obey and appeal to the authority over them.
- Know how to work together in unity.
- Are willing intercessors and fasting for our nation to return to God.
- Are not of a double mind—exposing sin, not winking at it.
- Are not of a fearful heart in spiritual warfare.

Chapter 23

A Prayer For
My Beautiful America

O America, My Beautiful America,
God has shed His grace on you.
He has blessed your shining shores.
He has blessed your grain fields with richness.
Your God, whom you have leaned on in the past, has made
    you rich.
He has fought your battles many times as you have leaned
    upon Him.

O America, My Beautiful America,
Nations have looked upon you with envy,
But it is time to again call upon your God.
America, you are leaving the paths you have once trod.

Shame is upon you for the rivers of pornography you are
    stooping in,
To fulfill the lust of the eye.
"When lust is conceived it produces the evils of sin,
Sin when it is finished brings forth death and lostness."
    (James 1:15)

Call upon your God, My America, while there is time to call,
For your God shall come, and he shall not tarry,
And His reward will be with Him.

The voices of many aborted souls are crying out for vindi-
    cation.
Oh America, My Beautiful America,
The blessing of many a soul,
Cry out forgiveness to your God,
He will hear your cry.

Shame is upon you, America.
Sodom and Gomorrah point an accusing finger at you,
For your liberties to homosexual practices.
Once they were ashamed and stayed hidden,
But now they have become flagrant and demanding of
    rights,
Rights that they do not under your God's law deserve.
Instead of calling them forth, America,
You should put them to shame and lead them to God's
    forgiveness,
And cleansing and to the help they need,
To be delivered from their shameful practices.

America, call to God about your broken homes,
And marriages that are pulled asunder.
Your strength is in united families and your God,
Who has never turned away,
But you are turning away from Him.

America, freedom has been your blessing,
But freedom of everything is an abomination to your God.
Cults of every kind are free to operate on your shores.
Worship of Satan, your enemy, worship of men,
Worship of all kinds of idols, take place in your beautiful
    land.

Pray for cleansing, My Beautiful America.
Call upon your merciful God.
He will fight your battles,
He will hear you, send His Spirit,
To inspire you and give you a new heart.

America, you have been known as a Christian nation,
And your land flowed with milk and honey for the needy
    ones.
But you are not the sweet smelling fragrance
To God's nostrils as in the past.

O America, the lives of your precious gems, your youth,
Your children, cry out to you for help.
Drugs, alcohol and sexual sins are running rampant among
    them.
Ungodly men and women are using your precious heritage,
To fill their unholy lust, for sexual gratification,
And their greed, for monetary gain.
Your God will hold you accountable, My beautiful America.

Instead of beauty you are producing ashes.

So, My Beautiful America, repent and call upon your God,
That He may send a mighty revival,
Before He comes and finds you still in your whoredoms,
And you will be doomed.

God says, "If my people which are called by my name,
Will humble themselves, and pray,
And seek My face, and turn from their wicked ways,
Then I will hear from heaven, and will forgive their sin,
And I will heal their land."   II Chronicles 7:14

Oh My Beautiful America, call upon your mighty God.
To you who reads, or hears,
This message is to you.[1]

Let's join our hearts in prayer to God for our land, using the
words of a beloved song:

                                        Georgia B. Hall

Chapter 24

There Are Answers

We must recognize our enemy.

A champion in America's fight against Communism, J. Edgar Hoover, Chief of the FBI, wrote much about Communism. His knowledge unmasked Communism for what it really is—tyranny, brutal, and terrifying, in which all would become slaves of the ruling elite.

The Communist myth . . . is cynically immoral, an abject disillusionment . . . because it professes to be the savior of mankind, the architect of an alluring paradise where injustice, misery and war will be abolished. In Communist society . . . rights are non-existent: concentration camps the symbol of justice; terror the order of the day.[1]

In what is pictured as a workers' paradise (Communism), slave labor is commonplace . . .

Communism is more than an economic, political, social or philosophical doctrine. It is a way of life; a false materialistic "religion." It would strip man of his belief in God, his heritage of freedom, his trust in love, justice, and mercy.

Here is a terrifying aspect of Communism . . . its effort to indoctrinate the rising generation, to mold these minds to the atheistic tenets of Marxism-Leninism, to make them mere soulless cogs of a brutal machine . . .[2]

In the regime which claims to have eliminated all discrimination, anti-Semitism is virtually official policy.[3]

The pretension that Communism stands for national independence is flagrantly contradicted by the **brutal sup-**

pressions of the uprisings in East Germany, Hungary (in the autumn of 1956), the invasion of Czechoslovakia in August, 1968, and Tibet *(and we add to that list, more recently the brutal suppression of the uprising in Poland and the invasion of Afghanistan).*

Solzhenitsyn demonstrated in his book, *Gulag*, that the invariable aim of the long bloodshedding terror is always the same: **consolidation of power and destruction of even potential enemies.**[4]

The Communist educational program continuously selects the best young minds, finances their schooling, trains them thoroughly for specific scientific careers, and offers powerful incentives to stimulate them to outstanding effort . . . the results are solid evidence that, for Communist purposes, their educational system is frighteningly effective.

In Communist thinking, education is directed only to train men's bodies and minds for their role for the state. Since Communism denies the existence of God, there is no time for men's souls.

The struggle waged in the Soviet Union against religion is not for ideological reasons, but for *power*. The dissenters are not put in psycho-prisons because the ideology is unable to refute their critical statements, but because they are expressing themselves *without* being asked to do so.

The Communist Party leaders of the Soviet Union are not interested in ideology but in *conformity of thought*. Or rather, they are not even interested in whether everybody thinks the way prescribed by the last party plenary session, but only that *they do not think at all.*[5]

Communism . . . by treason and trickery seeks to destroy this great Republic and force the United States of America to grovel under the absolute domination of a brutal philosophy.

American lives have been lost in valiant attempts to prevent the Communist takeover of countries such as Korea and Viet Nam, yet these were struggles we didn't win.

America is committed to stopping the spread of Communism in this hemisphere, yet we seem almost helpless to end the build-up of the Marxists threatening our own borders.

What is the answer?

How can America become strong and overcome these Communist forces?

There are answers, but only if God is on our side—or more correctly, if we are on God's side.

An early observer said, "America is great, because America is good. If America ceases to be good, she will cease to be great."

America must return to the standards upon which she was founded—*one nation under God*.

There are many moral issues at stake—issues we have never had to face in our history. A few of the issues are:

- Government funding of organizations who provide counselling for, referrals for, and performance of abortions. We must insist this funding cease.
- Freedom to educate your children at home, without government control.
- Freedom for our children to have Bible studies or Christian activities in their schools, the same as other clubs and groups.
- Freedom for *all* people to have Bible studies and prayer meetings anywhere, without fear of the government. government.
- Freedom to resist the National Education Association and the public schools when they impose homosexuality and other immoral values in the classroom. Freedom to protect our rights to change materials being taught, to prevent NEA control.
- Freedom to speak out, and insist on change in television programming. There must be a revival of ethical personal and social standards. In the book, *A Christian Manifesto*, a public television station in Washington, D.C. refused to show the film *Whatver Happened To The Human Race* or even to consider it because of its pro-life position on abortion. The excuse? "We can't program anything that presents only one point of view." At the same time public TV was running *Hard Choices*, a program totally *in favor* of abortion. We must insist on equal treatment, and the same rules.

WE HAVE BECOME OUR OWN ENEMY

We must remember it is God who has allowed all these problems to come upon our nation. We are facing situations and issues that seen insurmountable, but every one of them will become ineffective and melt away if America will turn back to our roots, and live according to God's Word.

Unless we hear the cry of repentance in our land, the judgment of God will get worse. He will raise up more enemies, and more deadly diseases, until we repent—or we are destroyed off our land.

The answer is clear—God is not finished with America yet, but America had better wake up!

Footnotes

Introduction
1. Oral White House briefing, February 3, 1986.

Chapter 1
1. Dr. D. James Kennedy, *Memorial Day Message*, May, 1985.

Chapter 4
1. J. Edgar Hoover, *Communism* (New York: Random House, XX), 133-134.
2. Ibid., 135.
3. Ibid., 30.

Chapter 5
1. *Family Protection Report* (Baltimore: Family Protection Lobby, 1982).
2. Dr. Samuel Blumenfeld, *NEA Trojan Horse in American Education* (Boise: Paradigm, 1984), 4.
3. Ibid., 5.
4. Ibid., 11.
5. Ibid., 8.
6. Edward Hitchcock, *Age of the Academies* (New York: Colombia University, 1964), 22.
7. Ibid., 1.
8. Ibid., 28-29.
9. National Education Association, *Fiftieth Anniversary Volume*, 335.
10. Robert McKay, *Chairman*, NEA Legislation Committee.
11. Blumenfeld, *Op. cit.*, 242.
12. *Education Week*, May 16, 1984.

Chapter 6
1. *U.S. Bureau of Education Report*, Washington: Bureau of Education, 1910.
2. James McKeen Cattell, *School and Society*, January 30, 1915, 179.
3. Blumenfeld, *Op cit.*, 102.
4. G. Stanley Hall, *Educational Problems.* (New York: 1911), 443-444.
5. "The University School" *Univer. Record*, 1896, 417-422.
6. Dr. Samuel T. Orton, cited in Blumenfeld, *Op cit.*, 110.
7. *Mayhew and Edwards, The Dewey School*, 142-143.
8. Dr. John Dewey, *Liberalism and Social Action* (New York: G.P. Putnam's Sons, 1935), 52.
9. Blumenfeld, *Op. cit.*, 130.
10. Blumenfeld, *Op. cit.*, 135.
11. Dr. Lewis A. Alesen, Mental Robots (Caldwell, ID: Caxton Printers, 1967), 73.
12. Blumenfeld, *Op. cit.*, 137.

Chapter 7

1. Blumenfeld, *Op. cit.*, 113.
2. *Life Magazine*, April, 1944.
3. Pollack & Martuza, "Teaching Reading in the Cuban Primary Schools," *Journal of Reading*, (December, 1981), 241-243.
4. Blumenfeld, *Op. cit.*, 135.
5. Blumenfeld, *Op. cit.*, 20.
6. *New York Times*, June 15, 1979.
7. *Education Week*, May 16, 1984.
8. *Intercessors Newsletter*, (Washington: Intercessors for America, January, 1986).
9. *CWA Newsletter*, (Washington: Concerned Women for America, December 1985).

Chapter 8

1. Dr. Francis A. Schaeffer, *A Christian Manifesto* (Westchester: Crossway, 1981), 54.
2. *Humanist Manifesto II* (American Humanist Association), 13.
3. Ibid., 16.
4. Ibid., 17.
5. Ibid., 18.
6. Ibid., 19.
7. Ibid., 21.
8. Ibid., 22.
9. Ibid., 23.
10. Ben Alexander, "Humanism" *Exposing Satan's Power*, Nov./Dec. 1985, 2.
11. Leonard LeSourd, *The Intercessors*, December, 1985, 4.

Chapter 9

1. C.C. Herriott, *It Can Happen Here* (Oradell, NJ: American Tract Society, No Date).
2. Ibid.,
3. Dr. Harney Klehr, *The Heyday of American Communism* (New York: Basic Books, 1984), 226.
4. Ibid., 194.
5. Ibid., 200.
6. Ibid., 257.
7. Ibid., 204.
8. Hoover, *Op cit.*, 148.
9. Ibid., 109.
10. American Tract Society, *Op cit.*
11. Ibid.
12. Hoover, *Op. cit.*, 56-58.

Chapter 10

1. George Sheldes, *The Great Thoughts* (New York: Ballantine, 1985), 240-241.
2. John Lenczowski, *White House Briefing*, November 7, 1985.

Chapter 11

1. James McKeever, *McKeener Strategy Letter*, October 8, 1985.
2. Ibid.
3. Don Kirk, "U.N.'s Critics in the U.S.," *U.S.A. Today*, November, 1985, 4.

Chapter 12

1. *Soviet Military Power*, (Washington: Department of Defense, 1985), 143.

2. *Cuban Armed Subversion-Aggression 1959-69* (Washington: White House Paper).
3. *BiPartisan Commission Report* (Washington: White House Paper, January 1984).
4. Ibid.
5. Ibid.
6. *The Soviet-Cuban Connection in Central America and the Caribbean*, (Washington: Department of Defense, March 1985), 32.
7. Ibid., 37.
8. Ibid., 39.
9. Ibid., 40.
10. Ibid., 41.
11. Ibid., 33.
12. Ibid., 35.
13. Ibid., 34.
14. Ibid., 38.
15. Ibid., 39.
16. Ibid., 46.

Chapter 13
1. *EEBM Focus* (Eastern European Bible Mission, Nov/Dec. 1985), 4.
2. *Response* (Christian Response International, July/August 1985), 1.

Chapter 14
1. *Defense: Our Critical Need in a Complex World* (Washington: Department of Defense, October, 1985), 12.
2. The Soviet-Cuban Connection in Central America and the Caribbean, (Washington: Department of Defense, March 1985).

Chapter 15
1. *Freedom Fighters in Nicaragua* (Washington: White House Paper, February, 1985).
2. *Sandinistas and Middle Eastern Radicals* (Washington: Department of State, August 1985), 1.
3. Ibid.
4. Ibid.
5. Ibid., 4.
6. Ibid., 6.
7. Ibid.
8. Ibid., 7.
9. Ibid.
10. Ibid.
11. Ibid.
12. Ibid., 8.
13. Ibid., 10.
14. Ibid.
15. Ibid., 12.
16. Ibid.
17. Ibid.
18. Ibid., 13.
19. Ibid.
20. Ibid.

Chapter 16
1. *The Soviet-Cuban Connection in Central America and the Caribbean.* (Washington: Department of Defense, March 1985).
2. Oliver North, White House Briefing, February 4, 1986.
3. Department of Defense, *Op. cit.*, 23.
4. "Religious Persecution of the Indians" *White House Digest*, February, 1984, 12.
5. "Soviet-Cuban Connection" *La Nacion* (October 16, 1984).
6. Ibid.

Chapter 17
1. *Grenada: A Failed Revolution* (Washington: Department of State), 11.
2. Ibid., 1.
3. Ibid., 13.
4. Ibid., 17.

Chapter 18
1. *Koinonia*, Mexico Report, Vol. 4 (Waldorf: Koinonia, Sept. 1985), 4-8.

Chapter 21
Hoover, *Op. cit.*, 120.

Chapter 22
1. Underground Notes, *Mikajlo Mikajlo* (trans. Maria and Christopher Juastic), (Kansas City: Sheed, Andrews & McMeel, 1976), 91.
2. Ibid.
3. Ibid.
4. Hoover, *Op. cit.* 72, 73, 108.
5. Underground Notes, *Op. cit.*, 89.

Chapter 24
1. Georgia B. Hall, Rt. 1, Box 124, Rockingham, NC 28379.

Before You Go

Subscribe to Bill and Nita's newsletter *The Beam* ($24 per year, add $6 for first class postage). Write 10004 Lomond Drive, Manassas, Virginia 22110.

Recommended Newsletters

Concerned Women for America, 122 C Street, NW, Suite 800, Washington, DC 20001.

Intercessors for America, P.O. Box 2639, Reston, Virginia 22090.

The Freedom Report, The Freedom Council, Virginia Beach, Virginia 23466.

Voice of Americanism, Dr. Steuart McBirnie, Box 90, Glendale, California 91209.

Nita's Other Books

- **Pillars of the Pentagon**
- **Alaskan Lady**
- **Pentagon Tidbits**
- **God's Plan—Enjoy Your Children**

are available at your local bookstore.

Bill and Nita are available to speak to your group. To arrange an engagement, call: (703) 368-9878

or write: 10004 Lomond Drive
                 Manassas, Virginia 22110